KNIT *Latvian* MITTENS

17 PROJECTS WITH TRADITIONAL LATVIAN PATTERNS TO KNIT

MOTOKO ISHIKAWA

CONTENTS

P.06 Mittens with Geometric Design

P.08 Squirrel and Woodland Mittens

P.10 Four-Leaf Clover Mittens

P.12 Blue Star Mittens

P.14 Mittens with Berry Design

P.16 Snowflake Neck Warmer and Mittens

P.20 Floral Hand Warmers

P.21 Chocolate Box Ankle Warmers

P.22 Cosy Winter Hand Warmers & Hat

P.24 Cat Hand Warmers

P.26 Ivy and Window Wrist & Leg Warmers

P.28 Scarf with Circle and Triangle Design

P.30 Miniature Mitten Ornaments

P.32 A Day in the Life of a Mitten Maker

P.34 Yarns Used in the Book

P.35 How to Knit Designs

P.36 Before Starting to Knit

P.84 Basic Techniques

PROJECT GALLERY

Mittens with Geometric Design
Project P. 06
Pattern P. 54

Squirrel Mittens
Project P. 08
Pattern P. 51

Woodland Mittens
Project P. 08
Pattern P. 56

Four-Leaf Clover Mittens
Project P. 10
Pattern P. 38

Blue Star Mittens
Project P. 12
Pattern P. 58

Mittens with Berry Design
Project P. 14
Pattern P. 60

Snowflake Neck Warmer
Project P. 16
Pattern P. 62

Snowflake Mittens
Project P. 16
Pattern P. 64

Floral Hand Warmers
Project P. 20
Pattern P. 66

Chocolate Box Ankle Warmers
Project P. 21
Pattern P. 68

Cosy Winter Hand Warmers
Project P. 22
Pattern P. 70

Cosy Winter Hat
Project P. 23
Pattern P. 72

Cat Hand Warmers
Project P. 24
Pattern P. 74

Ivy and Window Wrist Warmers
Project P. 26
Pattern P. 76

Ivy and Window Leg Warmers
Project P. 27
Pattern P. 78

Scarf with Circle and Triangle Design
Project P. 28
Pattern P. 80

Miniature Mitten Ornaments
Project P. 30
Pattern P. 82

INTRODUCTION

On chilly days, it can be a struggle to leave the comfort of your cosy home.

That's why I've created some mittens and accessories featuring knit designs that will add some excitement to your outdoor excursions.

As you work, you'll delight in watching the patterns take shape with each new row.

If you're unfamiliar with two-colour knitting, begin by testing out the patterns using fewer stitches. Try your hand at more complex designs in due course.

Even when using the same pattern, different knitters can create very different finished products.

Take your time and work diligently; there is great satisfaction in completing a project independently.

I hope that you enjoy knitting these designs. Don't be afraid to experiment with aspects such as yarn tension and floating technique.

Motoko Ishikawa

NO. 1

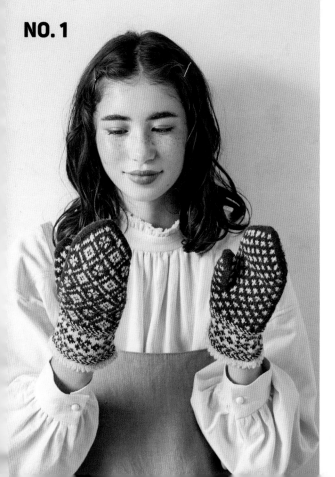

MITTENS WITH
GEOMETRIC DESIGN

A pair of mittens with a block-shaped geometric design inside a checkered pattern.

This may look tricky at first glance, but the knitting doesn't involve intertwining yarns that float a long way over the wrong side, making it an easy design to try.

These neatly and tightly woven mittens will keep the wind out, leaving you snug and warm.

INSTRUCTIONS / P.54
YARN / Jamieson's of Shetland Spindrift

NO. 2

NO. 3

SQUIRREL AND WOODLAND MITTENS

Mittens to put a smile on your face, with squirrels stuffing acorns into their cheeks.

I've designed these forest mittens with the idea of a squirrel habitat in mind.

Put the mittens together and a picture book world opens up before you.

INSTRUCTIONS / No.2 P.51, No.3 P.56
YARN / 2: Jamieson's of Shetland Spindrift
3: Hamanaka Sonomono Tweed

FOUR-LEAF CLOVER MITTENS

I've gone for a bold red for these mittens, which are designed around a four-leaf clover motif. I've included some of the basics of triangular mittens, including the knit, the picot edging and the arrow-like Kihnu Troi braided cast-on at the wrists, to give those of you who are new to these techniques a chance to master them.

INSTRUCTIONS / P.38 (step-by-step explanations with photographs)
YARN / DARUMA Shetland Wool

BLUE STAR MITTENS

The large star motif in royal blue is reminiscent of an icy winter sky. I've worked an intricate pattern into the palms of the hands, while the thumbs have snowflakes woven into them. It is a design full of intricate detail that is pleasing to the eye.

INSTRUCTIONS / P.58
YARN / Jamieson's of Shetland Spindrift

NO. 5

MITTENS WITH BERRY DESIGN

A pretty design of rows of berries. The wrist part has a tree leaf design. As you work, imagine stories of going to the woods in autumn to pick a basket full of berries.

INSTRUCTIONS / P.60
YARN / Jamieson's of Shetland Spindrift

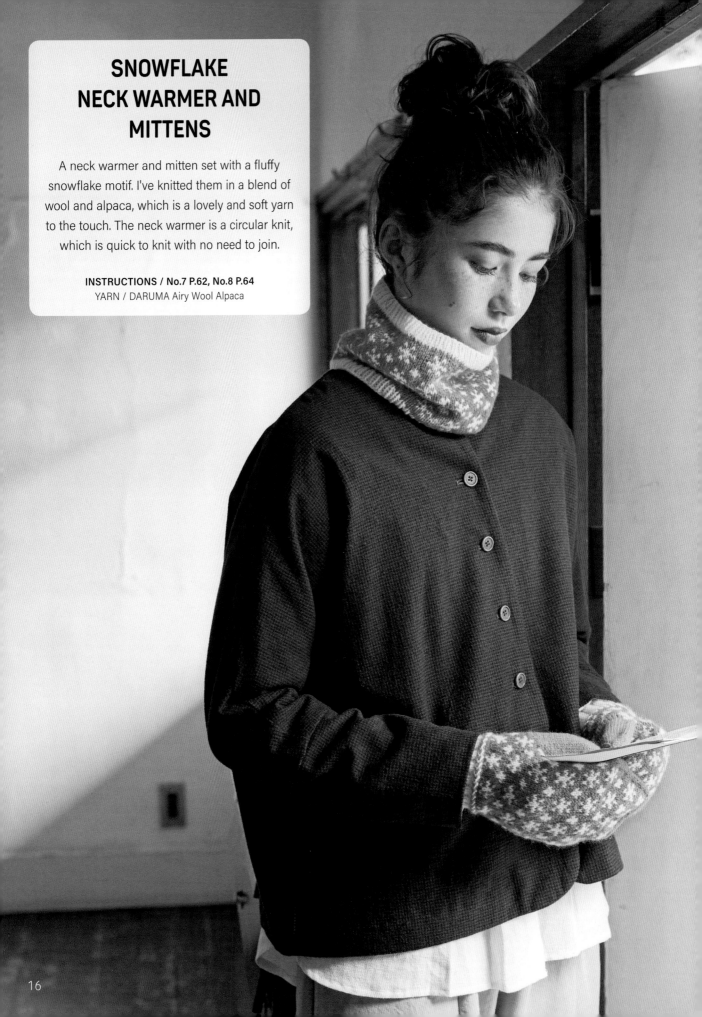

SNOWFLAKE NECK WARMER AND MITTENS

A neck warmer and mitten set with a fluffy snowflake motif. I've knitted them in a blend of wool and alpaca, which is a lovely and soft yarn to the touch. The neck warmer is a circular knit, which is quick to knit with no need to join.

INSTRUCTIONS / No.7 P.62, No.8 P.64
YARN / DARUMA Airy Wool Alpaca

NO. 7

NO. 8

Winter mittens to keep you warm and
happy on chilly outings.

mittens mittens mittens !

I have always been drawn to pretty triangle shapes. The tales behind each design are so captivating, you just want to whisper them to someone in confidence. As I work on my designs, I take time to reflect on fond memories, cherishing them in my heart.

FLORAL
HAND WARMERS

Navy petals with orange centers
as accents.
A layout featuring big, bold
flowers in rows it's uplifting just
to look at them.

INSTRUCTIONS / P.66
YARN / Jamieson's of Shetland Spindrift

NO. 9

CHOCOLATE BOX ANKLE WARMERS

I intended to knit a block pattern, but found it similar to having my favourite chocolates in a box.

Therefore, I named it the Chocolate Box pattern. The ankle warmers will be useful both indoors and outdoors, keeping your feet warm in the cold weather.

INSTRUCTIONS / P.68
YARN / Hamanaka Sonomono Tweed

NO. 10

COSY WINTER HAND WARMERS & HAT

A hat and hand warmer set displaying a winter scene of snowflakes covering the ground. Watch the design transform with each stage, creating an enjoyable anticipation to continue using it.

INSTRUCTIONS / No.11 P.70, No.12 P.72
YARN / DARUMA Airy Wool Alpaca

NO. 11

NO. 12

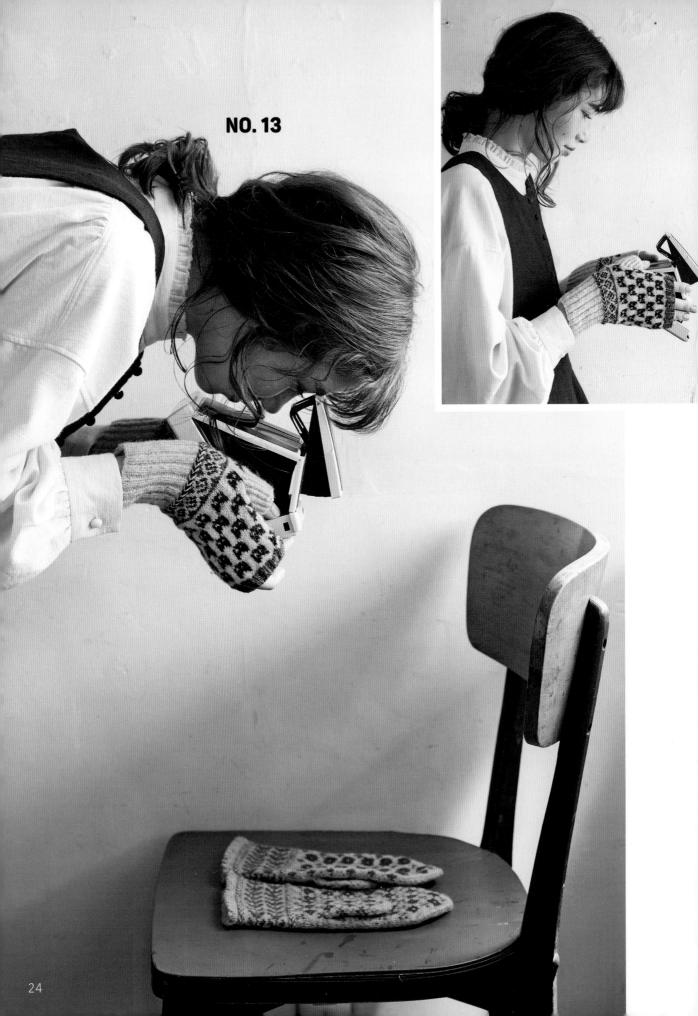

NO. 13

CAT HAND WARMERS

Here cat, cat...!
Hand warmers with many of my favorite patterns. Knitting in fashionable colours stops the design from appearing immature, instead adding a more advanced-and sophisticated look to it.

INSTRUCTIONS / P.74
YARN / Jamieson's of Shetland Spindrift

Wrist warmers are a useful and cosy accessory that you can wear even indoor.

They also enhance a plain outfit with a stylish touch.

IVY AND WINDOW WRIST & LEG WARMERS

I had a image in mind of ivy climbing freely around an old-fashioned window.
I wanted to depict both tranquility and motion, hence t he intricate pattern.
Take your time working on it steadily, and the feeling of accomplishment after completing
it will be immense.

INSTRUCTIONS / No.14 P.76, No.15 P.78
YARN / Jamieson's of Shetland Spindrift

These densely knitted leg warmers have excellent heat retention.

You will require some patience, but proceed gradually and cautiously.

SCARF with CIRCLE and TRIANGLE DESIGN

A scarf with a pattern made up of circles and triangles arranged in a rhythmic manner. Knitting in the round produces a thicker layer, resulting in increased warmth. When worn, it's enjoyable to see the design peeking through at random points.

I chose a simple colour scheme of navy and white on a gray base, with mustards accents.

INSTRUCTIONS / P.80
YARN / DARUMA Genmou Ni Chikai Merino Wool

NO. 16

a

b

INSTRUCTIONS / P.82

YARN

a / Hamanaka Sonomono Tweed

b, g, h, j, k / Jamieson's of Shetland Spindrift

c, i / DARUMA Shetland Wool

d, e / DARUMA Airy Wool Alpaca

f / DARUMA Genmou Ni Chikai Merino Wool

MINIATURE MITTEN ORNAMENTS

Miniature woolen mitten decorations can be knitted with leftover wool.
Enjoy creating various sizes and textures by altering the material and colours while keeping the number of rows and stitches the same. Little pieces are always lovely, and you'll undoubtedly want to make many of them!

d

e

f

k

h

i

j

g

A DAY IN THE LIFE OF A
MITTEN MAKER

My designs usually come from my everyday experiences.

I get inspiration from the different seasons, my trips, my tools, and my favourite things...

Anything that brings richness to my life as a mitten maker.

▲ A beautiful winter morning. The moon's face shining through the clouds is like a dream.

▼ A clear blue sky with tree shadows sharply etched onto the snow.

THE RICHNESS OF THE SEASONS

I reside in Hokkaido, a region of Japan overflowing with natural beauties. I enjoy the richness of the passing seasons that unfold before my eyes. All seasons possess gorgeousness, and I occasionally obtain inspiration for my creations from nature's tinges.

▲ My usual morning walking path. Walk in the season of fresh green.

▲ A bright red mushroom out of a storybook under a pine tree.

▲ The time of year when vibrant-coloured leaves fall to the ground.

TRAVEL

I've visited 18 countries until now. All of my trips have been unforgettable. One in particular that impressed me was to a craft fair in a forest near Riga, Latvia. The whole woodland was dedicated to the fair, and the stalls sold everything from gloves (naturally) to woodwork, textiles, ceramics, basketry, books and food.

▼ Baskets in various shapes and sizes!

◄ The food area had a lot to choose from, including traditional dishes from the Baltic region. Folks laid out blankets in the shadow of trees to share a picnic lunch.

◄ A museum that collects items such as ancient Estonian folk costumes, mittens and carpets and recreates knitting patterns to preserve them as valuable materials.

BOOKS AND TOOLS

I get ideas from old books on the subject when designing mittens. I use a computer for making the designs. I occasionally transfer the images from my mind to the computer without any preliminary sketches.

▲ Essential yarns for knitting gloves. I consistently keep available a selection of yarns from Jamieson's or that I've purchased at a yarn store.

▲ The first vintage book on Estonian mittens I came across is a treasured possession. It achieves an exquisite equilibrium between attractiveness and charm.

FAVORITE THINGS

There are two things that I cannot get through the day without - music and chocolate. I love to spend time with my teddy bears and cats.

▲ Vintage teddy bears I've collected over the years. They all look cute with their expressive faces.

▲ My cats. Even if they come to play while I'm working, it's pleasant and comforting to have their company.

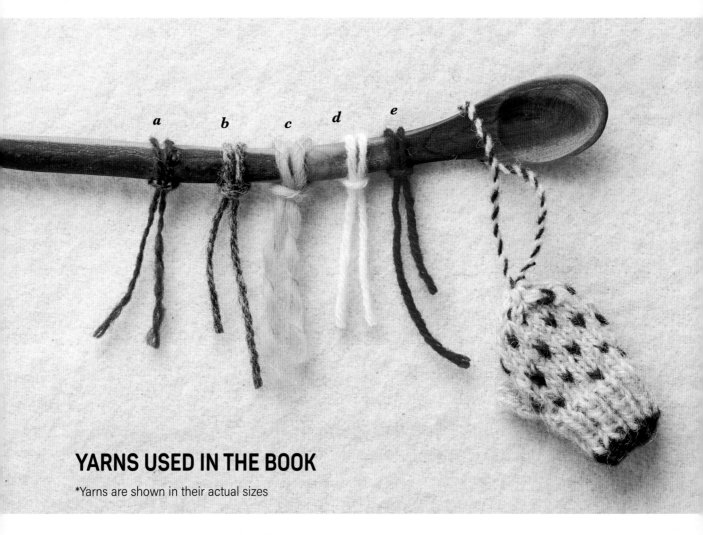

YARNS USED IN THE BOOK

*Yarns are shown in their actual sizes

a   **Jamieson's of Shetland Spindrift**

Wool (Shetland wool) 100% | 25-g Balls (approx. 105 m) | 225 Colors

Knitting Needles No. 3 (3.0 mm) to 5 (3.6 mm)

b   **Hamanaka Sonomono Tweed**

Wool 53%, Alpaca 40%, other (camel or yak) 7% | 40-g Balls (approx. 110 m) | 5 Colors

Knitting Needles No. 5 (3.6 mm) to 6 (3.9 mm)

c   **DARUMA Genmou Ni Chikai Merino Wool**

Wool (Merino) 100% | 30-g Balls (approx. 91 m) | 20 Colors

Knitting Needles No. 6 (3.9 mm) to 8 (4.5 mm)

d   **DARUMA Airy Wool Alpaca**

Wool (Merino) 80%, Alpaca Royal Baby Alpaca) 20% | 30-g Balls (approx. 100 m) | 13 Colors

Knitting Needles No. 5 (3.6 mm) to 7 (4.2 mm)

e   **DARUMA Shetland Wool**

Wool (Shetland wool) 100% | 50-g Balls (approx. 136 m) | 12 Colors

Knitting Needles No. 5 (3.6 mm) to 7 (4.2 mm)

LET'S ENJOY
KNITTING!

(**HOW TO KNIT DESIGNS**)

BEFORE STARTING TO KNIT

HOW TO READ THE CHARTS

Knitting Abbreviations

c = cm **CO** = cast on **inc** = increase **dec** = decrease

BO = bind off **rem** = remaining stitches **even** = work all stitches with no increases or decreases

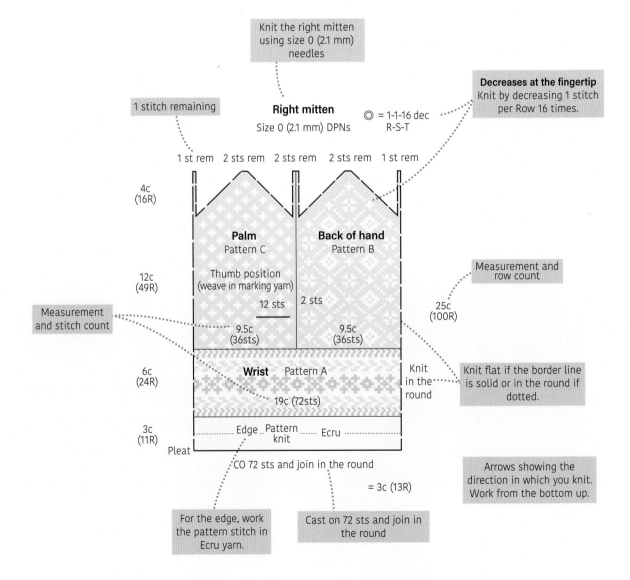

Knit the right mitten using size 0 (2.1 mm) needles

1 stitch remaining

Right mitten
Size 0 (2.1 mm) DPNs

◎ = 1-1-16 dec R-S-T

Decreases at the fingertip
Knit by decreasing 1 stitch per Row 16 times.

1 st rem   2 sts rem   2 sts rem   2 sts rem   1 st rem

4c (16R)

Palm
Pattern C

Back of hand
Pattern B

12c (49R)

Thumb position (weave in marking yarn)

12 sts

2 sts

Measurement and row count

25c (100R)

Measurement and stitch count

9.5c (36sts)

9.5c (36sts)

6c (24R)

Wrist   Pattern A

19c (72sts)

Knit in the round

Knit flat if the border line is solid or in the round if dotted.

3c (11R)

Edge   Pattern knit   Ecru

Pleat

CO 72 sts and join in the round

= 3c (13R)

For the edge, work the pattern stitch in Ecru yarn.

Cast on 72 sts and join in the round

Arrows showing the direction in which you knit. Work from the bottom up.

READING THE PATTERNS

How to read the patterns for flat knitting

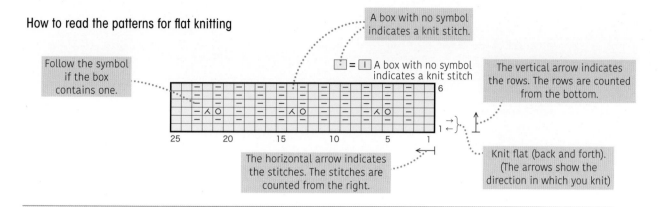

Follow the symbol if the box contains one.

A box with no symbol indicates a knit stitch.

⊡ = I A box with no symbol indicates a knit stitch

The vertical arrow indicates the rows. The rows are counted from the bottom.

The horizontal arrow indicates the stitches. The stitches are counted from the right.

Knit flat (back and forth). (The arrows show the direction in which you knit)

ABOUT GAUGES

The gauge indicates the density of the knit fabric in terms of the number of stitches and rows in 10 cm^2.

Gauges vary according to the knitter's hands, and there is no certainty that using the knitting needles specified in this book will produce the same measurements.

Make sure that you do a test knit to find the right gauge for you.

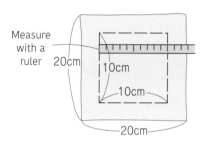

Measure with a ruler

20cm

10cm

10cm

20cm

Steam iron gently enough not to crush the stitches before you count the stitches in the 10 cm^2 area in the center.

Knit fabric made in a test knit

(Stitch sizes will be uneven in areas close to the edges of the knit, so knit 20 cm^2.)

Substitute with bulkier needles if there are more stitches and rows (tighter stitches) than the gauge specified in this book, and finer needles if there are fewer (looser stitches).

KNITTING FLAT AND IN THE ROUND

Knitting flat   Knit with two straight needles from one edge of the work to the other one row at a time looking alternately at the right and wrong sides.

Knitting in the round   Divide the stitches up among three of the four double pointed needles (or four of them if you have five needles), working in a tubular form with the remaining needle, always looking at the right side of the work.

Knitting pattern

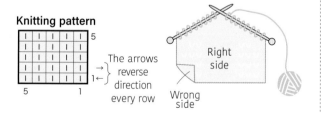

The arrows reverse direction every row

Right side

Wrong side

Knitting pattern

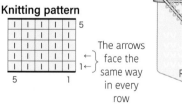

The arrows face the same way in every row

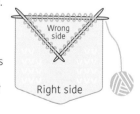

Wrong side

Right side

ABOUT THE KNITTING PATTERNS

The knitting patterns in the pieces featured in this book are all knitted **by the method of passing the yarn through to the wrong side.** Doubling the yarn through makes the knit fabric fuller, giving it better heat retention and robustness.

With items such as mittens and hand warmers, opting for smaller-sized needles than standard to work the patterns produces warmer pieces with denser knit fabric.

In the case of items where we want a softer finish such as neck warmers and hats, we work with different sizes of needle from mittens. The size of the needles can therefore change even for pieces with the same knit design. Make sure that you do a test knit (see P.43) to check the texture and softness of the work before you start knitting.

NO. 4 Page 11

YARNS USED
DARUMA Shetland Wool
Ecru (1) 35 g
Red (10) 30 g
Navy (5) 5 g

TOOLS
5 x size 2 (2.7 mm) double
pointed needles (DPNs)

GAUGE (10 cm²)
Patterns B, C 38 sts 35.5 rows

FINISHED SIZE
Palm circumference 20 cm
Length 24.5 cm

INSTRUCTIONS

1. Cast on in the standard way, work the mittens in the round using pattern stitch and patterns A to C, and then fasten off. Weave in a marking yarn at the thumb position part way round.

2. Pick up the stitch at the thumb position and undo the marking yarn, work the thumb in the round using pattern B, and then fasten off.

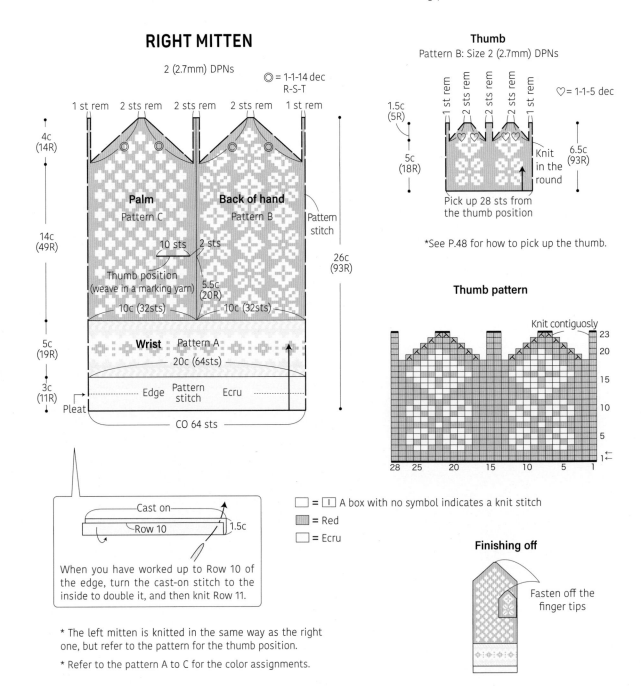

* The left mitten is knitted in the same way as the right one, but refer to the pattern for the thumb position.

* Refer to the pattern A to C for the color assignments.

MITTEN PATTERN

Knitting instructions are set out on pp. 40 to 50 with photographs for each step.

☐ = Ⅰ A box with no symbol indicates a knit stitch   ☐ = Ecru   ▦ = Red   ▨ = Navy

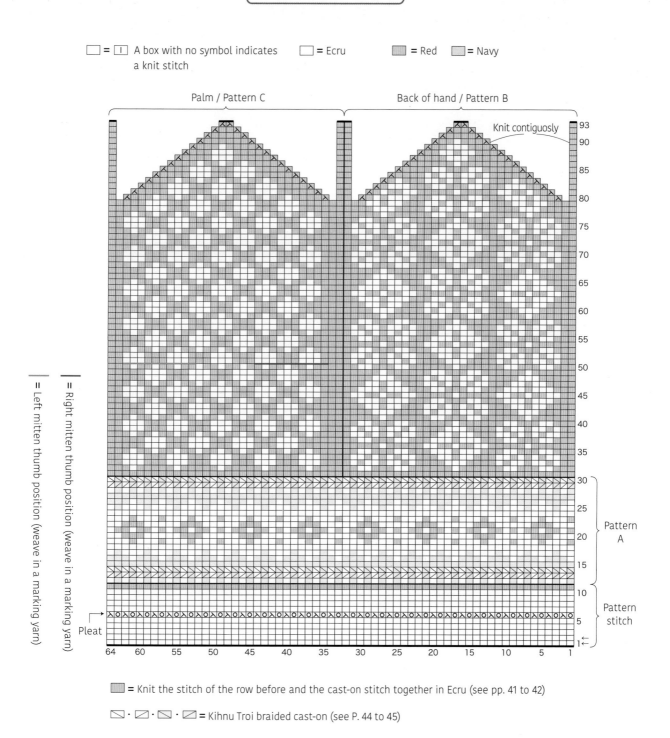

Palm / Pattern C   Back of hand / Pattern B

Knit contiguosly

Pattern A

Pattern stitch

Pleat

= Left mitten thumb position (weave in a marking yarn)

= Right mitten thumb position (weave in a marking yarn)

▦ = Knit the stitch of the row before and the cast-on stitch together in Ecru (see pp. 41 to 42)

◺ · ◹ · ◺ · ◹ = Kihnu Troi braided cast-on (see P. 44 to 45)

KNITTING THE MITTENS IN DESIGN NO.4

1. WORK THE EDGE

Rows 1 to 5

* The right mitten is demonstrated here.
* Different yarn color was used here to make things clearer.

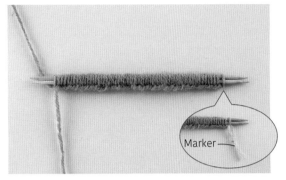

Marker

1 Cast on 64 stitches in the usual way, using two of the five double pointed needles. We will then place a marker at the first cast-on stitch using a marking yarn or other method.

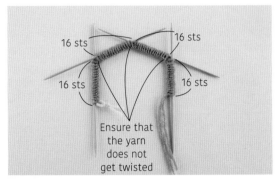

16 sts   16 sts

16 sts   16 sts

Ensure that the yarn does not get twisted

2 Divide the stitches up over the four double pointed needles (16 stitches on each.) This will be the first row.

3 Repeat the yarn over and SSK to work Row 6.

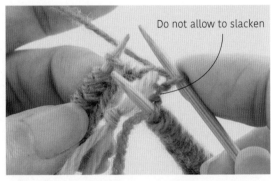

Do not allow to slacken

4 Work as far as Row 10 in knit stitch, following the pattern.

5 Work four rows in knit stitch (giving you five rows together with the cast-on stitches.)

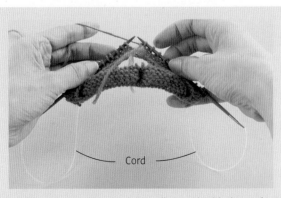

Cord

When knitting with circular needles, work with the cord pulled out to each side as shown in the photograph.

Row 6

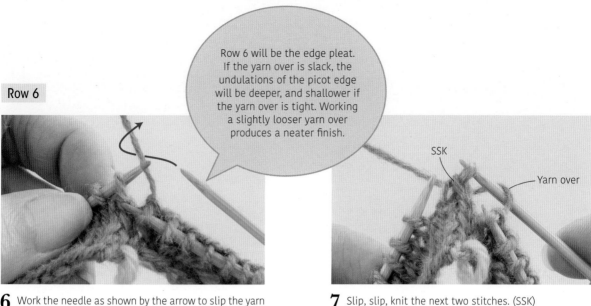

Row 6 will be the edge pleat. If the yarn over is slack, the undulations of the picot edge will be deeper, and shallower if the yarn over is tight. Working a slightly looser yarn over produces a neater finish.

SSK

Yarn over

6 Work the needle as shown by the arrow to slip the yarn onto the right-hand needle. (Yarn Over)

7 Slip, slip, knit the next two stitches. (SSK)

Rows 7 to 10

8 Repeat the yarn over and SSK to work Row 6.

9 Work as far as Row 10 in knit stitch, following the pattern.

Row 11   * I have changed the color of the cast-on yarn to make things clearer.

10 Turn the cast-on stitches over to the inside as shown by the arrow.

11 This is how it will look when you have turned the cast-on stitches over. Insert the needle into the stitch of the row before on the left-hand needle and the cast-on stitch as shown by the arrow and work the two knit stitches together.

The chain of cast-on stitches into which you insert the needle, seen from the right side.

12 This is how it will look when you have knitted one stitch. Work in the same way, inserting the needle as shown by the arrow.

13 Here, you have knitted two stitches. Repeat the instruction to knit the stitch of the row before and the cast-on stitch together to work Row 11.

If it is hard to put the needle into the chain of cast-on stitches, skip Row 11 without knitting it and blind stitch at the end. (See P.50.)

14 You have now knitted Row 11.

15 As seen from the wrong side.

2. KNITTING THE WRIST

Row 11

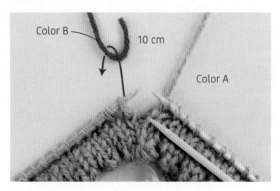

Color B

10 cm

Color A

1 Rest color A and work color B in knit stitch. Leave a tail of about 10 cm.

Color A is underneath

2 Here, you have made the knit stitch in color B. You will make the next stitch in color A. When you switch from color B to color A, work by bringing the yarn through so that color A goes under color B.

Color B is on top

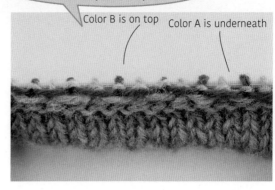

Here we have color A underneath and color B on top, but it's best to check the arrangement of the yarn when you do the test knit (see below.)

Color B is on top   Color A is underneath

3 You will make the next stitch in color B. When you switch from color A to color B, work by bringing the yarn through so that color B goes over the top of color A. Repeat steps 2 to 3, making alternate stitches of color A and color B one at a time.

* Leave some ease in the yarn when you bring it through, so that it doesn't get snagged on the wrong side.

4 You have now knitted Row 12. On the wrong side, the yarn is floating with color A underneath and color B on top, as shown in the photograph.

ARRANGING THE COLOR ASSIGNMENTS IN PATTERNS

The arrangement of the color assignments will appear differently depending on the feel of the person doing the knitting. It's a good idea to do a test knit to check which color looks nicest brought through on top and choose the arrangement that works best for you.

A. A test knit with the green yarn coming through on top. The design shows up nicely.

RS

WS

B. A test knit with the white yarn coming through on top. The areas with the white yarn are sunken, and the design does not show up as clearly.

RS

WS
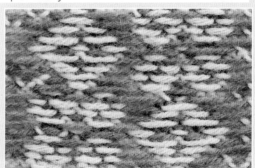

The above example is purely for reference.
It may well be that arranging the colors the other way round looks nicer, so always do a test knit to get the gauge and be sure.

Rows 13 to 14: Kihnu Troi Braided Cast on

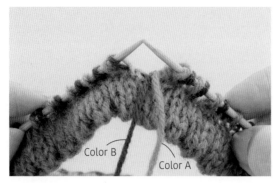

5 In Row 13, you will purl by twisting the A and B color yarns around each other. Bring the A and B color yarns to the front of the work.

6 Bring color B through under color A and purl in color B.

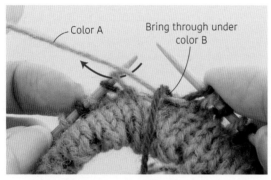

7 Continue by bringing color A through under color B and purling in color A.

8 Repeat steps 6 to 7, making alternate stitches of color A and color B one at a time. Always bring the color you are working through under the color you are not working when purling.

9 The yarns will soon become twisted up as you work, so undo the twists from time to time before you knit on.

10 You have now knit Row 13. The yarns that you have brought through to the front of the work will be flowing from top right to bottom left.

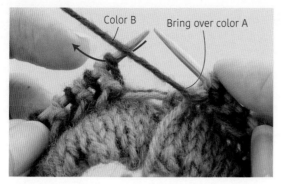

Color B   Bring over color A

11 For Row 14, bring the yarn through the opposite way to the row before. Purl by bringing color B through over color A.

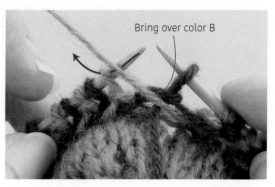

Bring over color B

12 Continue by bringing color A through over color B and purling in color A. Purl by bringing the color you are knitting through over the color you are not knitting.

13 You have now knitted Row 14. The yarns that you have brought through to the front of the work will be flowing from top left to bottom right. Bring the A and B color yarns through to the other side of the work.

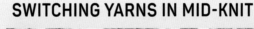

Rows 15 to 30

14 Knit the wrist, following the pattern.

SWITCHING YARNS IN MID-KNIT

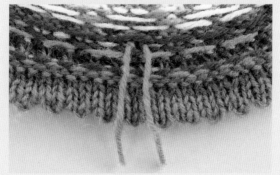

When switching yarns in mid-knit, do not tie the yarn off, but knit on, leaving a tail of about 10 cm as shown in the photograph.

3. KNITTING THE PALM AND BACK OF THE HAND

Rows 31 to 50

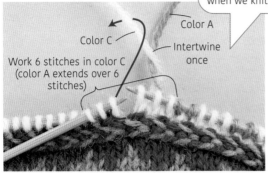

If you intertwine the yarn once, the arrangement of the yarns will be reversed. We will correct the arrangement when we knit the next color.

Color C
Color A
Intertwine once
Work 6 stitches in color C (color A extends over 6 stitches)

Intertwine different places

1 Knit pattern B and C. In Row 32, there is a place at which color A floats six stitches. If you knit on without doing anything here, this area will catch when you put the mitten on, so intertwine once in mid-work. In the same way, also intertwine once in mid-work in any section where the color assignment yarn or foundation yarn floats five stitches or more.

2 If you are entwining the yarn in two or more consecutive rows, make sure you do so in different places.

Rows 51 to 79

Marking yarn

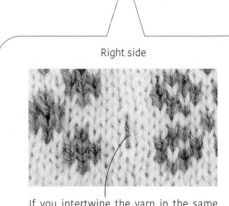

Right side

If you intertwine the yarn in the same place, the yarn that floats is more likely to show up on the right side.

3 In Row 51, knit a marking yarn at the thumb position. Knit 34 stitches using patterns B and C, and then make ten knit stitches with a marking yarn when you get to the thumb position. Leave a tail of about 10 cm in the marking yarn so that it can't unravel.

4 Return the 10 stitches you made in step 3 to the left-hand needle.

5 Knit over the stitches you made in the marking yarn once more with Pattern C. Continue by knitting as far as Row 79, following the pattern.

Rows 80 to 93

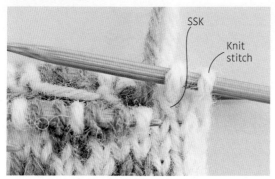

6 Do a decrease at the fingertip. In Row 80, work one knit stitch and then slip, slip, knit (SSK) the next two stitches. Continue by making 26 stitches to knit pattern B.

7 For the next two stitches, knit two together (k2tog). Work one knit stitch to create a decrease on the back of the hand. Do a decrease in the palm in the same way.

Fastening off * I have changed the color of the yarn to make things clearer.

8 Knit as far as Row 93, following the pattern.

9 Cut the yarn leaving a tail of 15 cm, thread it through the wool needle, and pass it twice through the remaining eight stitches.

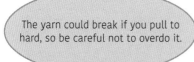

The yarn could break if you pull to hard, so be careful not to overdo it.

13 Pull the yarn through and fasten. Insert a wool needle into the work through the center of the closure as shown by the arrow and pull the tail out to the wrong side.

4. KNITTING THE THUMBS

Pick-Up Stitches

1 Start picking up from the stitch marked [STAR], following the pattern on the right. You will pass the four needles through a total of 28 stitches, as shown in the photograph.

2 Pull the marking yarn out.

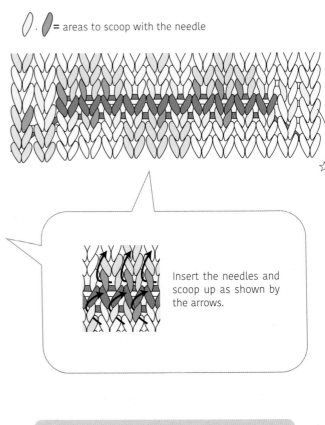

⬭ . ⬮ = areas to scoop with the needle

Insert the needles and scoop up as shown by the arrows.

> By picking up the stitches on the outside of the thumb position in this way too, we make that there are no holes at the base of the thumb.

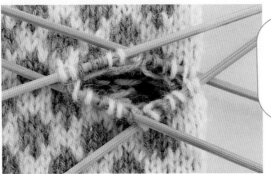

3 Here, we have picked up 28 stitches from the thumb position.

Row 1 * I have changed the color of the yarn to make things clearer.

4 Work the first row. This is how it will look when you have worked 14 knit stitches at the bottom, starting from the stitch marked [STAR]. Insert the needle as shown by the arrow when doing stitch 15.

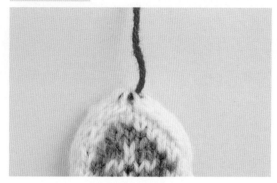

5 This is how it will look when you have worked seven knit stitches at the top. Insert the needle through the remaining seven stitches and work the knit stitches in the same way.

6 Knit as far as Row 23, following the pattern. As you did with the mitten, thread the yarn through the remaining eight stitches and fasten, and then bring the tail through to the wrong side. This completes the thumb.

5. FINISHING OFF

Weaving In The Yarn Tail

1 Turn the mitten out to the wrong side, thread the yarn tail onto the wool needle, and pass it through the wrong-side stitches about 3 cm horizontally, without the yarn tail showing through on the wrong side. Make sure that there are no splits on the right side.

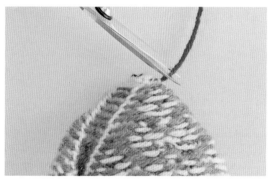

2 Cut the yarn just off the edge of the work.

> Passing the yarn tail through vertically would make it easier for the finger tips to touch the yarn. Passing the yarn tail through horizontally makes it harder to touch the yarn, which in turn makes the mittens more comfortable to wear.

3 Do the same with yarn ends in mid-knit: pass the needle through horizontally, weaving the yarn tail in without it showing through on the wrong side. The right mitten is now finished. Knit the left mitten in the same way.

DOUBLING THE EDGE WITH BLIND STITCH

* Double in this way if Row 11 of the edge is difficult to knit neatly.

Skip Row 11 of the edge without knitting, knit the mitten and thumb all the way through, and then fasten off. It's a good idea to turn the cast-on stitches back onto the inside at the pleat in Row 6 of the edge and stitching on in a natural position.

* I have changed the color of the cast-on stitch and blind stitch to make things clearer.

Soaking

Soaking produces a softer finish.

Do as follows to soak the mittens.

1. Press the mitten gently in lukewarm water containing a neutral detergent and rinse.

2. Squeeze the knit fabric and place between a dry towel to remove the water.

3. Shape and dry flat.

Ironing

You can also finish the piece by steaming it with an iron. Always use a protective cloth to ensure that the steam does not come into direct contact with the knit fabric.

This is how they look on completion

The finished mittens

YARNS USED
Jamieson's of Shetland Spindrift
Dark Brown (Espresso) (970) 35 g
Ecru (Eesit/White) (120) 20 g
Green (Leaf) (788) 5 g

TOOLS
5 x size 0 (2.1 mm) double pointed
needles (DPNs)

GAUGE (10 cm²)
Patterns B, C 38 sts 40 rows

FINISHED SIZE

Palm circumference 19 cm
Length 23.5 cm

INSTRUCTIONS

1. Cast on in the standard way, work the
mittens in the round using pattern stitch
and patterns A to C, and then fasten off.
Weave in a marking yarn at the thumb position part way round.

2. Pick up the stitch at the thumb position and undo the marking yarn, work the
thumb in the round using pattern D, and
then fasten off.

RIGHT MITTEN

Size 0 (2.1 mm) DPNs

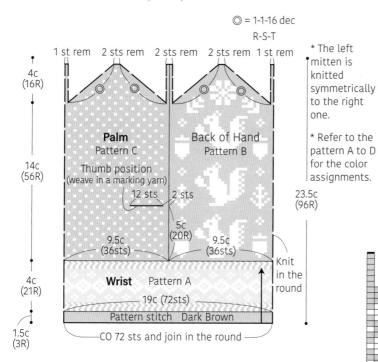

◎ = 1-1-16 dec
R-S-T

* The left
mitten is
knitted
symmetrically
to the right
one.

* Refer to the
pattern A to D
for the color
assignments.

Thumb

Pattern D   Size 0 (2.1 mm) DPNs

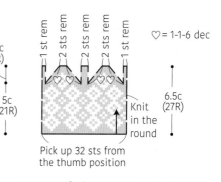

♡ = 1-1-6 dec

*See pp.48 for how to pick up the thumb.

Finishing off

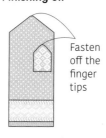

Fasten
off the
finger
tips

* Continued on the next page.

Thumb Pattern

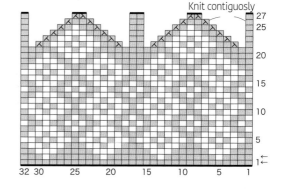

Knit contiguosly

☐ = I A box with no symbol indicates a knit stitch
▨ = Dark Brown
☐ = Ecru

LEFT MITTEN PATTERN

□ = Ⅰ A box with no symbol indicates a knit stitch   ▨ = Dark Brown   □ = Ecru   ▨ = Green

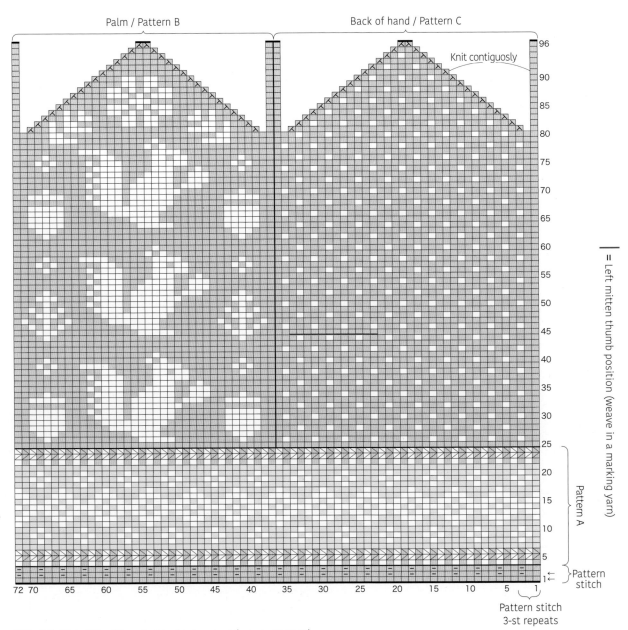

Palm / Pattern B   Back of hand / Pattern C

Knit contiguosly

96
90
85
80
75
70
65
60
55
50
45
40
35
30
25
20   Pattern A
15
10
5
1   Pattern stitch

= Left mitten thumb position (weave in a marking yarn)

72 70   65   60   55   50   45   40   35   30   25   20   15   10   5   1

Pattern stitch
3-st repeats

▨ · ▨ · □ · ▨ = Kihnu Troi braided cast-on (see pp. 44 to 45)

RIGHT MITTEN PATTERN

□ = I A box with no symbol indicates a knit stitch   ▨ = Dark Brown   □ = Ecru   ▨ = Green

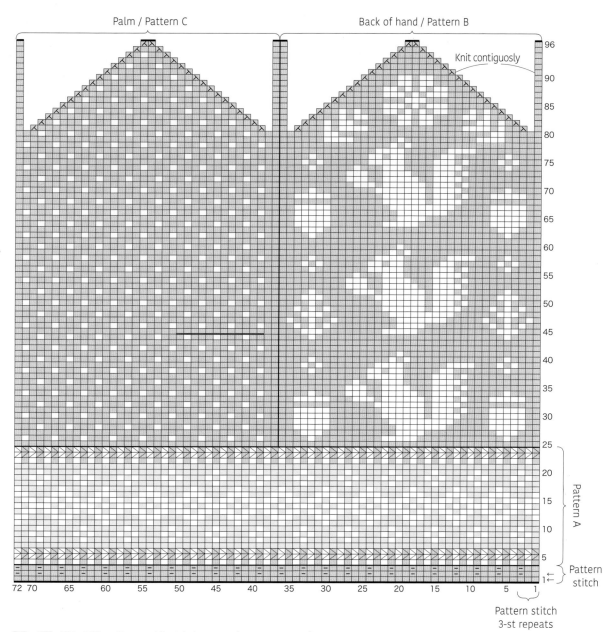

Palm / Pattern C   Back of hand / Pattern B

Knit contiguosly

= Right mitten thumb position (weave in a marking yarn)

Pattern A

Pattern stitch

Pattern stitch
3-st repeats

◨ · ◩ · ◺ · ◿ = Kihnu Troi braided cast-on (see pp. 44 to 45)

NO. 1 Page 6

YARNS USED
Jamieson's of Shetland Spindrift
Ecru (Eesit/White) (120) 25 g
Dark Green (Pine Forest) (292) 25 g
Brown (Peat) (198) 5 g

TOOLS
5 x size 0 (2.1 mm) double pointed
needles (DPNs)

GAUGE (10 cm²)
Patterns B, C 38 sts 40.5 rows

FINISHED SIZE
Palm circumference 19.5 cm Length 23.5 cm

INSTRUCTIONS
1. Cast on in the standard way, work the
mittens in the round using pattern stitch and
patterns A to C, and then fasten off. Weave
in a marking yarn at the thumb position part
way round.

2. Pick up the stitch at the thumb position and
undo the marking yarn, work the thumb in the
round using pattern C, and then fasten off.

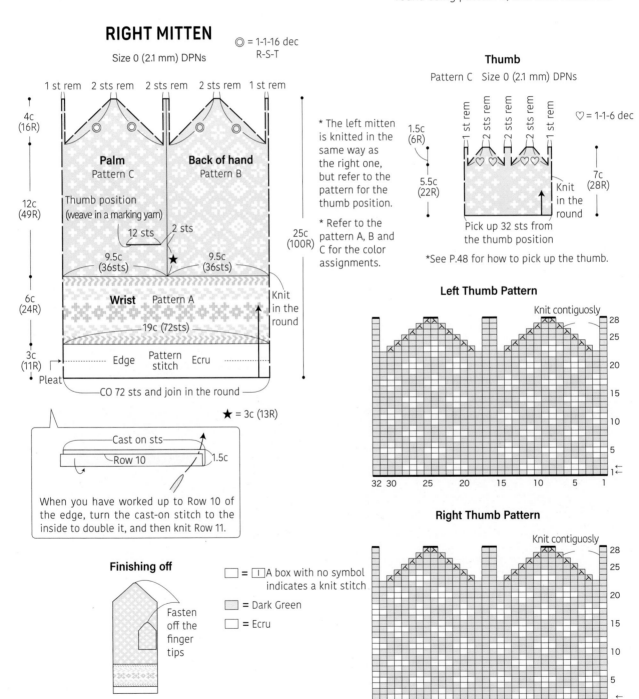

* The left mitten is knitted in the same way as the right one, but refer to the pattern for the thumb position.

* Refer to the pattern A, B and C for the color assignments.

*See P.48 for how to pick up the thumb.

When you have worked up to Row 10 of the edge, turn the cast-on stitch to the inside to double it, and then knit Row 11.

Finishing off

Fasten off the finger tips

☐ = Ⅰ A box with no symbol indicates a knit stitch

▨ = Dark Green

☐ = Ecru

MITTEN PATTERN

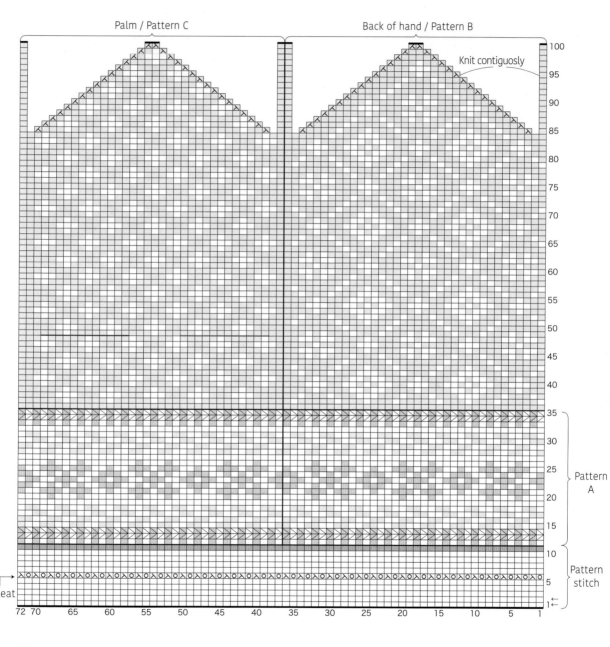

▨ = Knit the stitch of the row before and the cast-on stitch together in Ecru yarn (see pp. 41 to 42).

◺ · ◿ · ◣ · ◢ = Kihnu Troi braided cast-on (see pp. 44 to 45)

YARNS USED
Hamanaka Sonomono Tweed
Ecru (71) 45 g
Brown (73) 30 g

TOOLS
5 x size 1 (2.4 mm) double pointed needles (DPNs)

GAUGE (10 cm²)
Patterns B, C 30 sts 32 rows

FINISHED SIZE
Palm circumference 20 cm Length 24 cm

INSTRUCTIONS
1. Cast- on in the standard way, work the mittens in the round using pattern stitch and patterns A to C, and then fasten off. Weave in a marking yarn at the thumb position part way round.

2. Pick up the stitch at the thumb position and undo the marking yarn, work the thumb in the round with stockinette stitch, and then fasten off.

RIGHT MITTEN

Size 1 (2.4 mm) DPNs

◎ = 1-1-13 dec
R-S-T

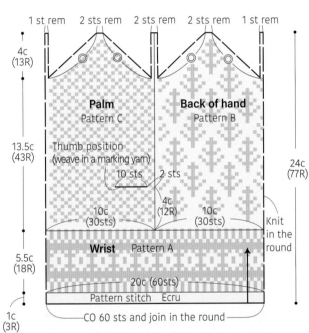

* The left mitten is knitted in the same way as the right one, but refer to the pattern for the thumb position.

* Refer to the pattern A, B and C for the color assignments.

Thumb
Stockinette stitch
Ecru   Size 1 (2.4 mm) DPNs

♡ = 1-1-5 dec

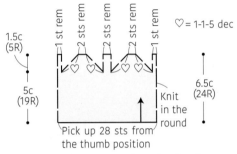

Pick up 28 sts from the thumb position

*See P.48 for how to pick up the thumb.

Thumb Pattern

□ = I A box with no symbol indicates a knit stitch

Knit contiguosly

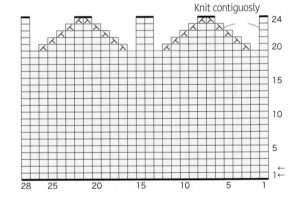

Finishing off

Fasten off the finger tips

MITTEN PATTERN

☐ = □ A box with no symbol indicates a knit stitch   ☐ = Ecru   ▨ = Brown

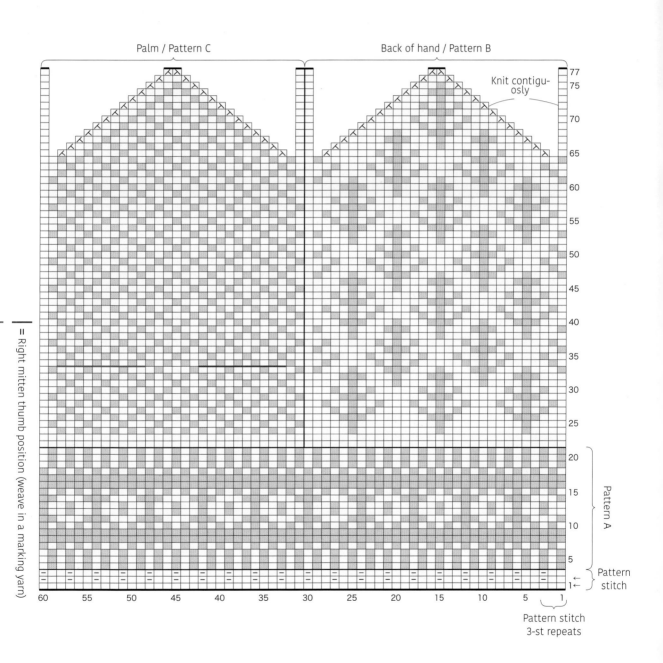

NO. 5 Page 12

YARNS USED
Jamieson's of Shetland Spindrift
Ecru (Eesit/White) (120) 40 g
Blue Royal (700) 25 g

TOOLS
5 x size 0 (2.1 mm) double pointed
needles (DPNs)

GAUGE (10 cm²)
Patterns B and C 38 sts 39.5 rows

FINISHED SIZE
Palm circumference 19 cm Length 25 cm

INSTRUCTIONS
1. Cast on in the standard way, work the mittens in the round using pattern stitch, patterns A to C, and 1 x 1 twisted rib, and then fasten off. Weave in a marking yarn at the thumb position part way round.

2. Pick up the stitch at the thumb position and undo the marking yarn, work the thumb thround using pattern D, and then fasten off.

RIGHT MITTEN

Size 0 (2.1 mm) DPNs

◎ = 1-1-16 dec
R-S-T

1 st rem   2 sts rem   2 sts rem   2 sts rem   1 st rem

4c (16R)

Palm
Pattern C

Back of hand
Pattern B

Knit in the round

15.5c (61R)

Pattern A

12 sts   2 sts

Thumb position (weave in a marking yarn)

6c (24R)

26.5c (107R)

9.5c (36sts)   9.5c (36sts)

0.5c (2R)

3c (15R)

Wrist   1x1 twisted rib   Ecru

0.5c (2R)

3c (11R)

Edge   Pattern stitch   Ecru

Pleat

CO 72 sts and join in the round

★ = 19c (72sts)

Cast on sts
Row 10
1.5c

When you have worked up to Row 10 of the edge, turn the cast-on stitch to the inside to double it, and then knit Row 11.

* The left mitten is knitted in the same way as the right one, but refer to the pattern for the thumb position.

* Refer to the pattern A to D for the color assignments.

1.5c (6R)

6c (23R)

Thumb
Pattern D   Size 0 (2.1 mm) DPNs

1 st rem   2 sts rem   2 sts rem   2 sts rem   1 st rem

♡ = 1-1-6 dec

♡ ♡ ♡   ♡ ♡ ♡

7.5c (29R)

Knit in the round

Pick up 32 sts from the thumb position

*See P.48 for how to pick up the thumb.

Left Thumb Pattern

Knit contiguosly

29
25
20
15
10
5
1

32 30   25   20   15   10   5   1

☐ = ☐ A box with no symbol indicates a knit stitch

☐ = Ecru

▨ = Blue

Finishing off

Fasten off the finger tips

MITTEN PATTERN

= A box with no symbol indicates a knit stitch   = Ecru   = Blue

Palm / Pattern C   Back of hand / Pattern B

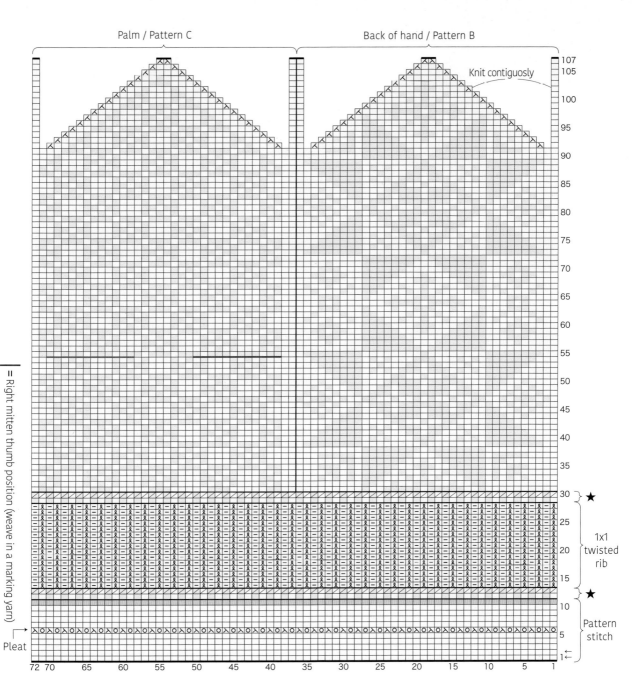

Knit contiguosly

107
105
100
95
90
85
80
75
70
65
60
55
50
45
40
35
30 } ★
25
20   1x1
      twisted
15   rib
10 } ★
      Pattern
5   stitch
1 }

= Left mitten thumb position (weave in a marking yarn)

= Right mitten thumb position (weave in a marking yarn)

Pleat →

72 70 65 60 55 50 45 40 35 30 25 20 15 10 5 1

= Knit the stitch of the row before and the cast-on stitch together in Ecru yarn (see pp. 41 to 42).

· = Kihnu Troi braided cast-on (see pp. 44 to 45)

★ = Pattern A

YARNS USED
Jamieson's of Shetland Spindrift
Beige (Eesit) (105) 40 g
Dark Pink (Redcurrant) (572) 10 g
Blue Green (Sage) (766) 10 g
Khaki (Wren) (246) 5 g

TOOLS
5 x size 0 (2.1 mm) double pointed needles (DPNs)

GAUGE (10 cm²)
Patterns B, C 38 sts 39.5 rows

FINISHED SIZE
Palm circumference 19 cm Length 24 cm

INSTRUCTIONS

1. Cast on in the standard way, work the mittens in the round using pattern stitch and patterns A to C, and then fasten off. Weave in a marking yarn at the thumb position part way round.

2. Pick up the stitch at the thumb position and undo the marking yarn, work the thumb in the round using pattern C, and then fasten off.

RIGHT MITTEN

Size 0 (2.1 mm) DPNs

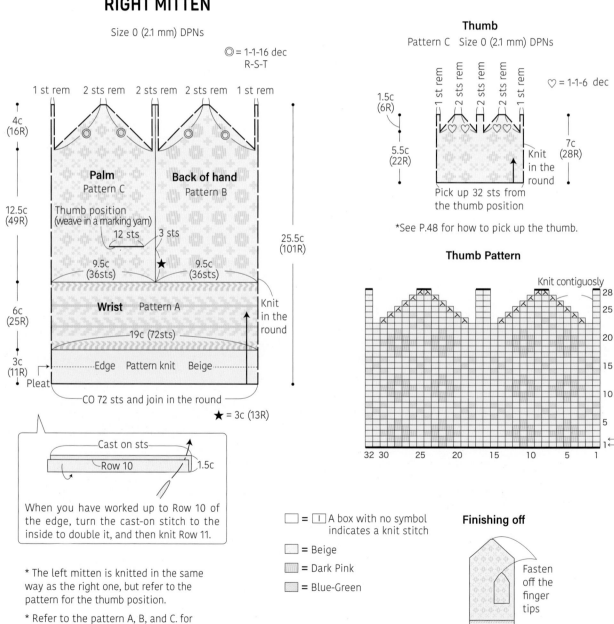

◎ = 1-1-16 dec R-S-T

1 st rem   2 sts rem   2 sts rem   2 sts rem   1 st rem

4c (16R)

Palm
Pattern C

Back of hand
Pattern B

Thumb position (weave in a marking yarn)

12 sts   3 sts

12.5c (49R)

9.5c (36sts)   ★   9.5c (36sts)

25.5c (101R)

Wrist   Pattern A

Knit in the round

6c (25R)

19c (72sts)

3c (11R)

Edge   Pattern knit   Beige

Pleat

CO 72 sts and join in the round

★ = 3c (13R)

Cast on sts
Row 10
1.5c

When you have worked up to Row 10 of the edge, turn the cast-on stitch to the inside to double it, and then knit Row 11.

* The left mitten is knitted in the same way as the right one, but refer to the pattern for the thumb position.

* Refer to the pattern A, B, and C. for the color assignments.

Thumb
Pattern C   Size 0 (2.1 mm) DPNs

♡ = 1-1-6 dec

1.5c (6R)

1 st rem   2 sts rem   2 sts rem   2 sts rem   1 st rem

5.5c (22R)

Knit in the round

7c (28R)

Pick up 32 sts from the thumb position

*See P.48 for how to pick up the thumb.

Thumb Pattern

Knit contiguosly

28
25
20
15
10
5
1

32 30   25   20   15   10   5   1

☐ = 𝕀 A box with no symbol indicates a knit stitch

☐ = Beige

▨ = Dark Pink

☐ = Blue-Green

Finishing off

Fasten off the finger tips

MITTEN PATTERN

□ = I A box with no symbol indicates a knit stitch   □ = Beige   ▨ = Khaki   ▨ = Blue-Green   ▨ = Dark Pink

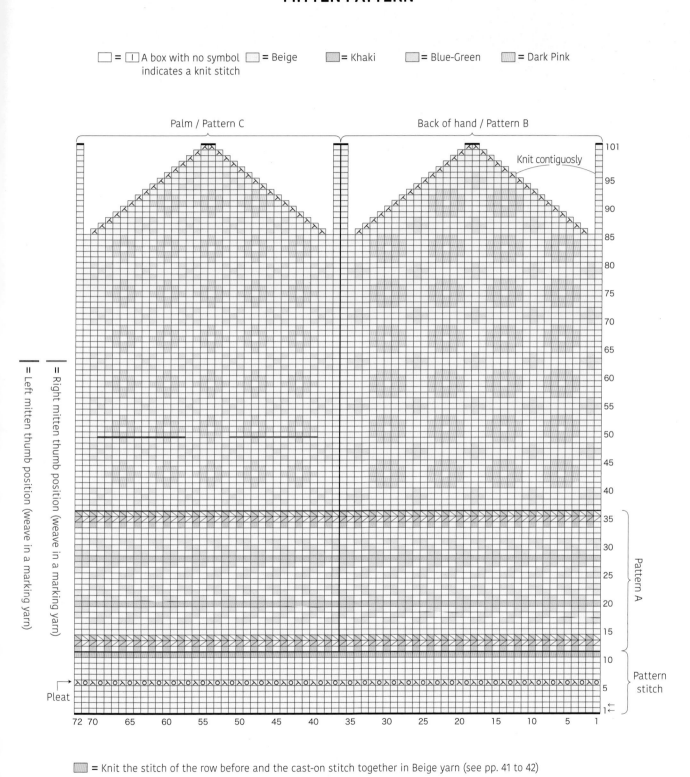

= Left mitten thumb position (weave in a marking yarn)

= Right mitten thumb position (weave in a marking yarn)

Palm / Pattern C

Back of hand / Pattern B

Knit contiguosly

Pattern A

Pattern stitch

Pleat

▨ = Knit the stitch of the row before and the cast-on stitch together in Beige yarn (see pp. 41 to 42)

��️ · ◲ · ◳ · ◱ = Kihnu Troi braided cast-on (see pp. 44 to 45)

NO. 7 Page 16

YARNS USED
DARUMA Airy Wool Alpaca
Blue Gray (5) 20 g
Ecru (1) 15 g

TOOLS
4 x size 6 (3.9 mm) double pointed needles (DPNs) and

1 x size 4 (3.3 mm) DPN or straight needle (for binding off)

GAUGE (10 cm²)
Pattern 24 sts 29.5 rows

FINISHED SIZE
Circumference 50 cm Length 15 cm

INSTRUCTIONS
Cast on in the standard way, work the neck warmer in the round with 1 x 1 ribbing and the knit pattern, and then bind off.

NECK WARMER PATTERN

☐ = Ⅰ A box with no symbol indicates a knit stitch   ☐ = Ecru   ☐ = Blue-Gray

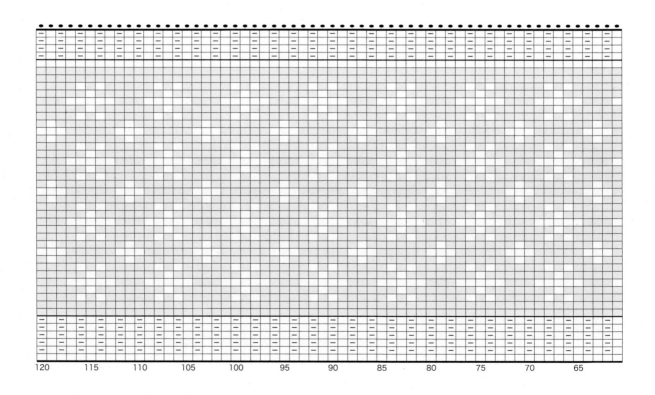

120   115   110   105   100   95   90   85   80   75   70   65

NECK WARMER

Size 6 (3.9 mm) DPNs

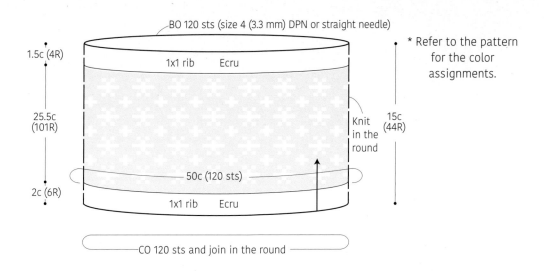

* Refer to the pattern for the color assignments.

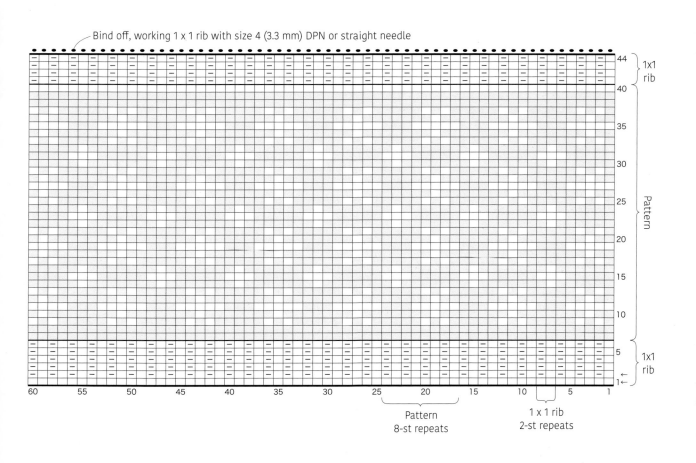

NO. 8 Page 16

YARNS USED
DARUMA Airy Wool Alpaca
Blue Grey (5) 30 g
Ecru (1) 25 g

TOOLS
5 x size 2 (2.7 mm) double pointed
needles (DPNs)
5 x size 0 (2.1 mm) DPNs

GAUGE (10 cm²)
Pattern B 32 sts 33 rows

FINISHED SIZE
Palm circumference 20 cm Length 26 cm

INSTRUCTIONS
1. Cast on in the standard way, work the mittens
in the round using 2 x 2 rib and patterns A and
B, and then fasten off. Weave in a marking
yarn at the thumb position part way round.

2. Pick up the stitch at the thumb position and
undo the marking yarn, work the thumb in the
round using stockinette stitch, and then fasten off.

RIGHT MITTEN

Size 2 (2.7 mm) DPNs

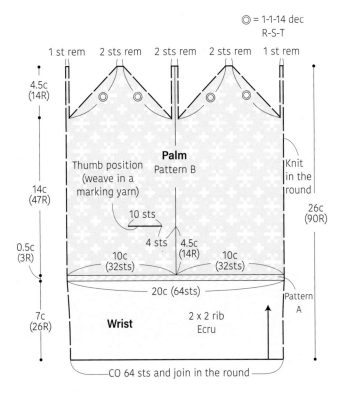

Thumb
Stockinette stitch
Blue-Gray   Size 0 (2.1 mm) DPNs

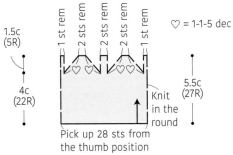

*See P.48 for how to pick up the thumb.

Thumb Pattern

☐ = ☐ A box with no symbol
indicates a knit stitch

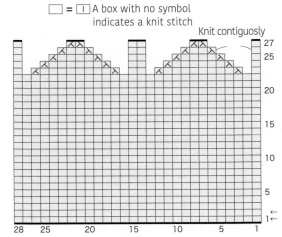

* The left mitten is knitted in the same way as the
right one, but refer to the pattern for the thumb
position.

* Refer to the pattern A and B for the color
assignments.

Finishing off

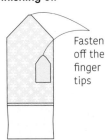

Fasten
off the
finger
tips

MITTEN PATTERN

☐ = ⊡ A box with no symbol
indicates a knit stitch   ☐ = Ecru   ▨ = Blue-Gray

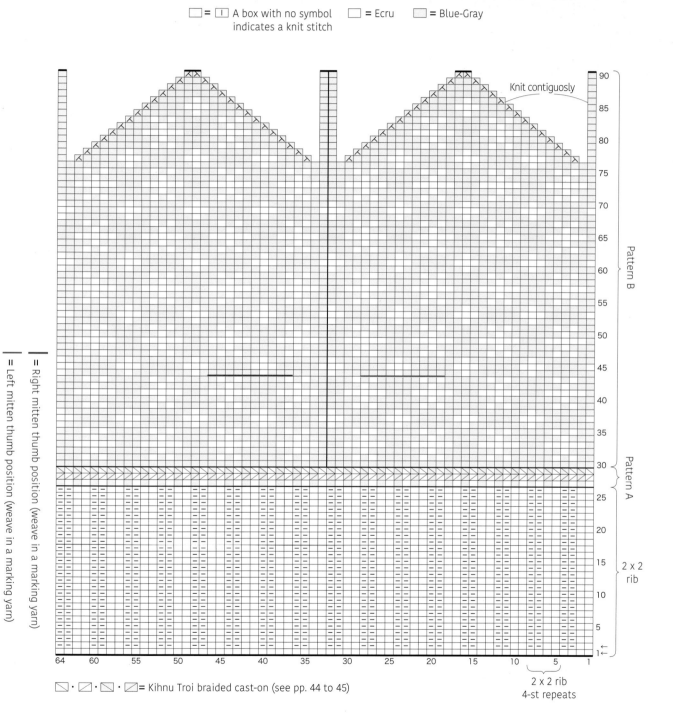

Knit contiguosly

Pattern B

Pattern A

2 x 2 rib

2 x 2 rib
4-st repeats

= Right mitten thumb position (weave in a marking yarn)

= Left mitten thumb position (weave in a marking yarn)

◨ · ◪ · ◨ · ◪ = Kihnu Troi braided cast-on (see pp. 44 to 45)

YARNS USED

Jamieson's of Shetland Spindrift
Light brown (Mooskit) (106) 35 g
Dark Navy (Dark Navy) (730) 15 g
Orange (Ginger) (462) 5 g

TOOLS

5 x size 0 (2.1 mm) double pointed
needles (DPNs)

GAUGE (10 cm²)

Pattern B 38 sts 41 rows

FINISHED SIZE

Palm circumference 20 cm Length 26 cm

INSTRUCTIONS

1. Cast on in the standard way and work the
hand warmers in the round using pattern
stitch and patterns A and B, and then bind
off. Weave in a marking yarn at the thumb
position part way round.

2. Pick up the stitch at the thumb position and
undo the marking yarn, work the thumb in the
round with 1 x 1 rib, and then bind off.

RIGHT HAND WARMER

Size 0 (2.1 mm) DPNs

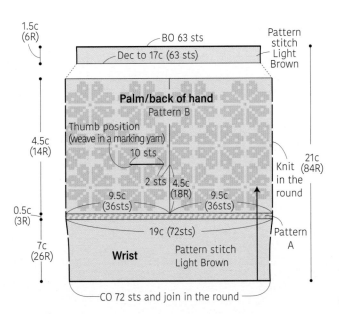

* The left handwarmer is knitted in the same
way as the right one, but refer to the pattern for
the thumb position.

* Refer to the pattern A and B for the color
assignments.

Thumb

1x1 rib
Light Brown   Size 0 (2.1 mm) DPNs

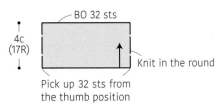

*See P.48 for how to pick up the thumb.

Thumb pattern

□ = ⊡ A box with no symbol
indicates a knit stitch

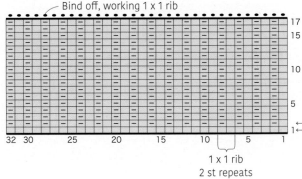

HAND WARMER PATTERN

☐ = ⊞ A box with no symbol indicates a knit stitch   ▨ = Light Brown   ▨ = Orange   ▨ = Dark Navy

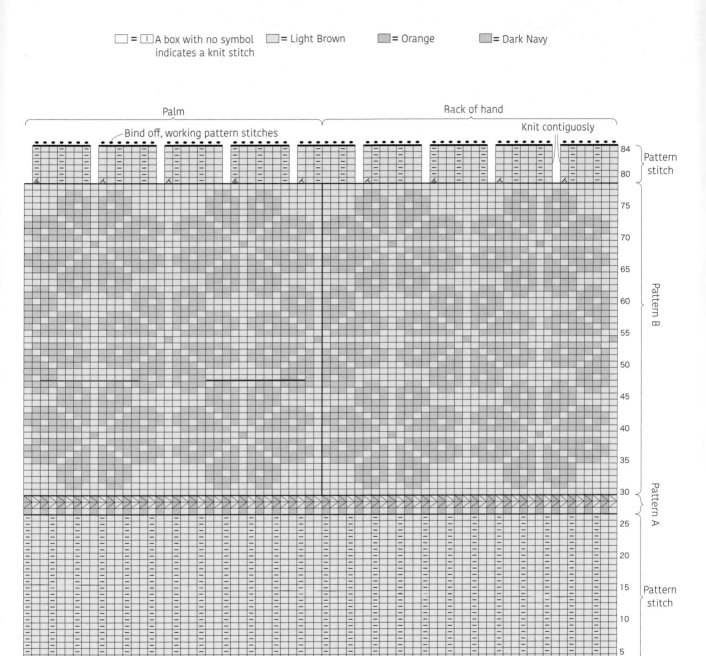

—— = Right mitten thumb position (weave in a marking yarn)
—— = Left mitten thumb position (weave in a marking yarn)

◤ · ◹ · ◣ · ◿ = Kihnu Troi braided cast-on (see pp. 44 to 45)

NO. 10 Page 21

YARNS USED
Hamanaka Sonomono Tweed
Ecru (71) 50 g
Charcoal Gray (75) 25 g

OTHER MATERIALS
Buttons (approx. 16-mm diameter) x 8

TOOLS
2 x size 1 (2.4 mm) double pointed
needles (DPNs),
1 x size 0 (2.1 mm) DPN or straight
needle (for binding off)

GAUGE (10 cm²)
Pattern 27.5 sts 31 rows

FINISHED SIZE
Ankle circumference 30 cm Length 16 cm

INSTRUCTIONS
1. Cast on in the standard way, work the
main section in the round using pattern
stitch and the pattern, and then bind off.

2. Pick up the stitches from the main
section, work edges A, A', and B in pattern
stitch, and bind off.

3. Attach the buttons.

MAIN SECTION

Size 1 (2.4 mm) DPNs

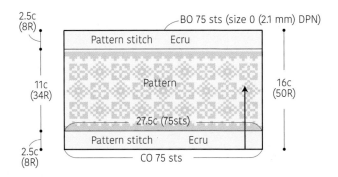

*Refer to the pattern for the color assignments.

Edge (left leg)
Pattern stitch   Ecru
Size 1 (2.4 mm) DPNs

Edge (right leg)
Pattern stitch   Ecru
Size 1 (2.4 mm) DPNs

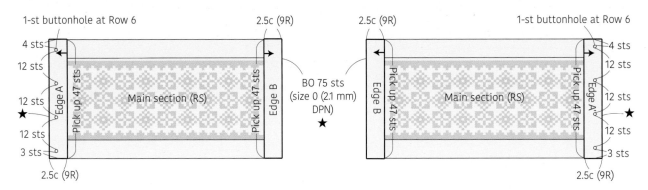

MAIN SECTION PATTERN

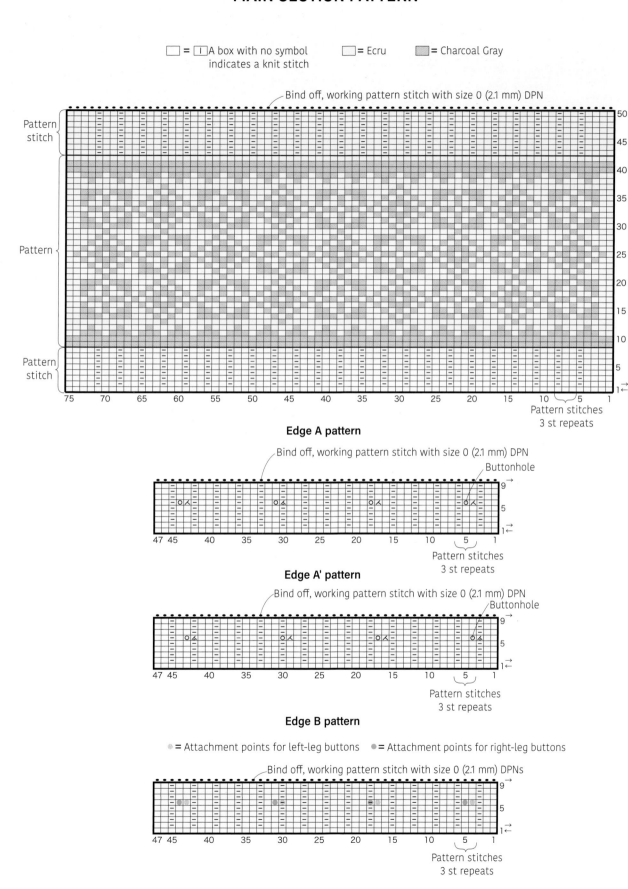

☐ = ☐ A box with no symbol indicates a knit stitch   ☐ = Ecru   ▨ = Charcoal Gray

Bind off, working pattern stitch with size 0 (2.1 mm) DPN

Pattern stitch

Pattern

Pattern stitch

75 70 65 60 55 50 45 40 35 30 25 20 15 10 5 1

Pattern stitches
3 st repeats

Edge A pattern

Bind off, working pattern stitch with size 0 (2.1 mm) DPN

Buttonhole

47 45 40 35 30 25 20 15 10 5 1

Pattern stitches
3 st repeats

Edge A' pattern

Bind off, working pattern stitch with size 0 (2.1 mm) DPN

Buttonhole

47 45 40 35 30 25 20 15 10 5 1

Pattern stitches
3 st repeats

Edge B pattern

● = Attachment points for left-leg buttons   ● = Attachment points for right-leg buttons

Bind off, working pattern stitch with size 0 (2.1 mm) DPNs

47 45 40 35 30 25 20 15 10 5 1

Pattern stitches
3 st repeats

NO. 11 Page 22

YARNS USED
DARUMA Airy Wool Alpaca
Navy (6) 35 g
Ecru (1) 15 g

TOOLS
5 x size 2 (2.7 mm) double pointed
needles (DPNs) and

1 x size 1 (2.4 mm) DPN or straight
needle (for binding off)

GAUGE (10 cm²)
Pattern A 32 sts 41 rows
Pattern B 32 sts 35.5 rows

FINISHED SIZE
Palm circumference 20 cm Length 21.5 cm

INSTRUCTIONS
1. Cast on in the standard way and work
the hand warmers in the round using
pattern stitch and patterns A and B. Make
the buttonholes by flat knitting as you
go along.

2. Bind off to finish.

HAND WARMERS

Size 2 (2.7 mm) DPNs

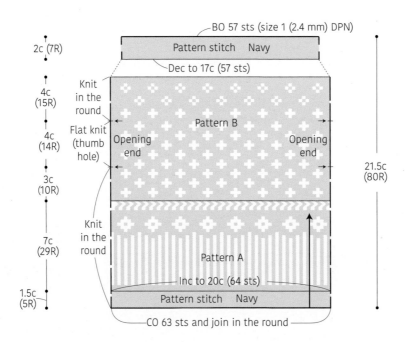

* Refer to the pattern A and B for the color assignments.

HAND WARMER PATTERN

□ = Ⅰ A box with no symbol indicates a knit stitch   ☒ = Make 1   ▨ = Navy   □ = Ecru

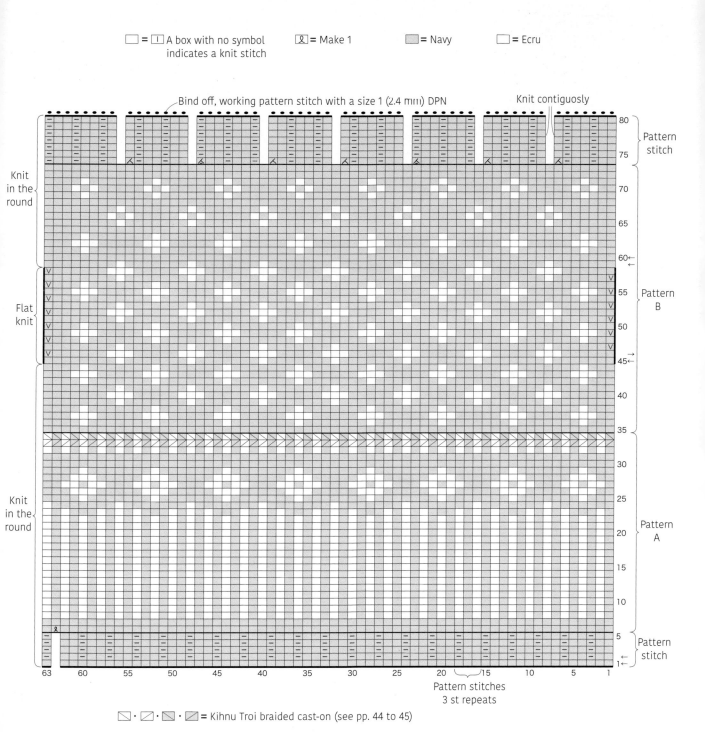

Bind off, working pattern stitch with a size 1 (2.4 mm) DPN

Knit contiguosly

Knit in the round

Flat knit

Knit in the round

Pattern stitch

Pattern B

Pattern A

Pattern stitch

80
75
70
65
60←
55
50
45←
40
35
30
25
20
15
10
5
1←

63 60 55 50 45 40 35 30 25 20 15 10 5 1

Pattern stitches
3 st repeats

◨ · ◪ · ◨ · ◪ = Kihnu Troi braided cast-on (see pp. 44 to 45)

Ⅴ = Do the first stitch in each row of the flat-knit section (Rows 46 to 58) as a slip stitch

71

NO. 12 Page 23

YARNS USED
DARUMA Airy Wool Alpaca
Navy (6) 50 g
Ecru (1) 10 g

TOOLS
4 x size 4 (3.3 mm) double pointed
needles (DPNs)

GAUGE (10 cm²)
Pattern A 29.5 sts 33 rows
Pattern B 29.5 sts 30 rows
Stockinette stitch 29.5 sts 40 rows

FINISHED SIZE
Head circumference 46 cm

INSTRUCTIONS
1. Cast on in the standard way, work the hat
in the round using 2 x 2 rib, patterns A and B,
and stockinette stitch, and then fasten off.

2. Make the pompom and attach it to the top.

HAT PATTERN

□ = ① A box with no symbol   □ = Navy   □ = Ecru
indicates a knit stitch

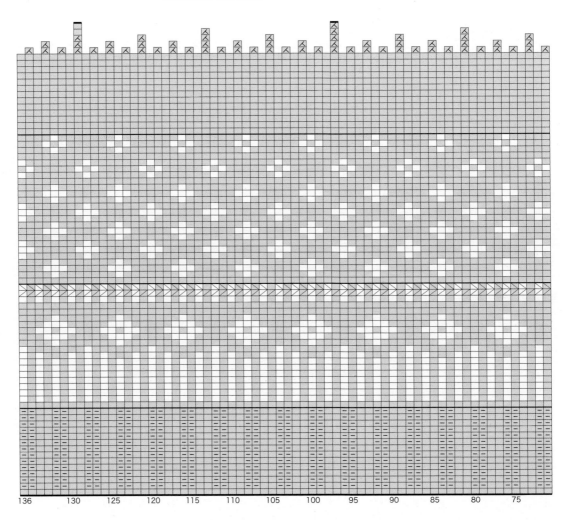

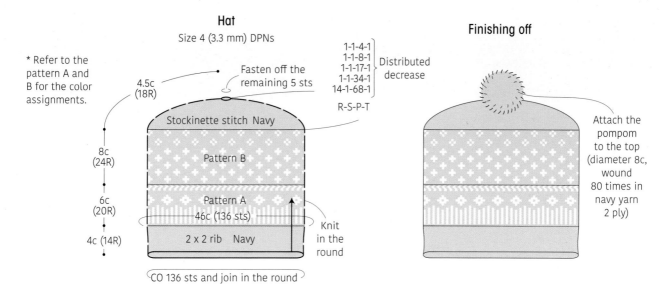

Hat
Size 4 (3.3 mm) DPNs

* Refer to the pattern A and B for the color assignments.

4.5c (18R)

Fasten off the remaining 5 sts

1-1-4-1
1-1-8-1
1-1-17-1
1-1-34-1
14-1-68-1

Distributed decrease

R-S-P-T

8c (24R)

6c (20R)

4c (14R)

Stockinette stitch Navy

Pattern B

Pattern A
46c (136 sts)

2 x 2 rib   Navy

Knit in the round

CO 136 sts and join in the round

Finishing off

Attach the pompom to the top (diameter 8c, wound 80 times in navy yarn 2 ply)

◻ · ◿ · ◨ · ◿ = Kihnu Troi braided cast-on (see pp. 44 to 45)

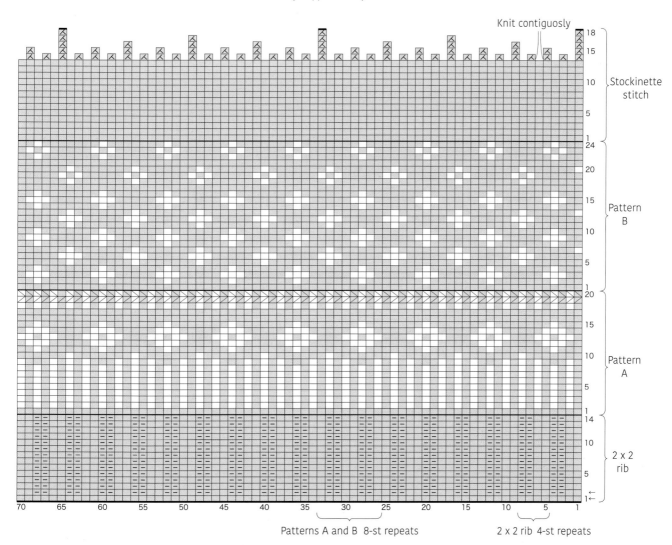

Knit contiguosly

Stockinette stitch

Pattern B

Pattern A

2 x 2 rib

Patterns A and B 8-st repeats   2 x 2 rib 4-st repeats

YARNS USED
Jamieson's of Shetland Spindrift
Ecru (Eesit/White) (120) 30g
Black (Shetland Black) (101) 10g
Dark Brown (Moorit/Shaela) (118) 5g

TOOLS
5 x size 0 (2.1 mm) double pointed needles (DPNs)

GAUGE (10 cm²)
Pattern B 38 sts 40 rows

FINISHED SIZE
Palm circumference 19 cm Length 19 cm

INSTRUCTIONS
1. Cast on in the standard way, work the hand warmers in the round using 2 x 2 rib and patterns A and B, and then bind off. Weave in a marking yarn at the thumb position part way round.

2. Pick up the stitch at the thumb position and undo the marking yarn, work the thumb in the round with 1 x 1 twisted rib, and then bind off.

RIGHT HAND WARMER

Size 0 (2.1 mm) DPNs

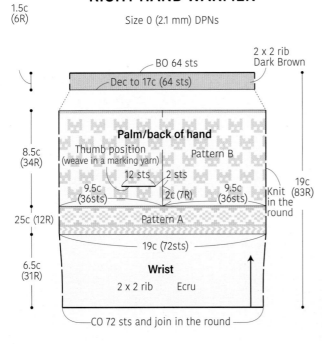

Thumb
1x1 twisted rib
Ecru   Size 0 (2.1 mm) DPNs

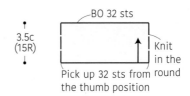

*See P.48 for how to pick up the thumb.

Thumb Pattern

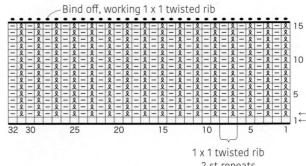

1 x 1 twisted rib
2 st repeats

* The left hand warmer is knitted in the same way as the right one, but refer to the pattern for the thumb position.

* Refer to the pattern A and B for the color assignments.

RIGHT HAND WARMER PATTERN

☐ = ⊡ A box with no symbol indicates a knit stitch   ☐ = Ecru   ▧ = Black   ▨ = Dark Brown

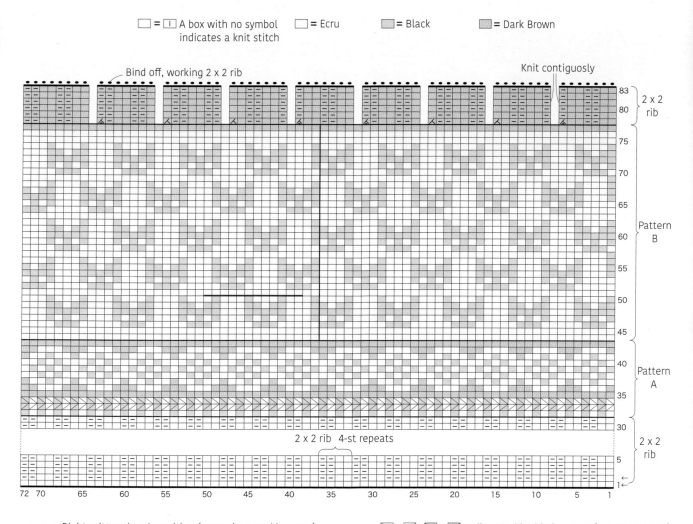

— = Right mitten thumb position (weave in a marking yarn)
— = Left mitten thumb position (weave in a marking yarn)

◹ · ◺ · ◹ · ▨ = Kihnu Troi braided cast-on (see pp. 44 to 45)

PATTERN B ON THE LEFT HAND WARMER

* The same as the right hand warmer except for pattern B.

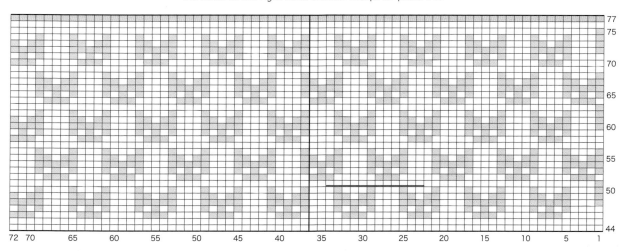

YARNS USED

Jamieson's of Shetland Spindrift

Navy (Admiral Navy) (727) 15 g

Gray (Sholmit) (103) 10 g

Off White (Natural White) (104) 10g

Chocolate (Moorland) (195) 10 g

TOOLS

5 x size 2 (2.7 mm) double pointed
needles (DPNs),

1x size 0 (2.1 mm) DPN or straight
needle

GAUGE (10 cm²)

Patterns A and B 33.5 sts 35.5 rows

FINISHED SIZE

Palm circumference 20 cm Length 21.5 cm

INSTRUCTIONS

Cast on in the standard way, work the wrist
warmers in the round using pattern stitch
and patterns A and B, and then bind off.

WRIST WARMERS

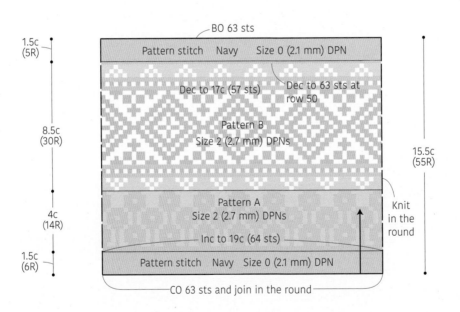

* Refer to the pattern A and B for the color assignments .

WRIST WARMER PATTERN

□ = □ A box with no symbol indicates a knit stitch ⚹ = Make 1 ▨ = Navy ▨ = Gray □ = Off White ▨ = Chocolate

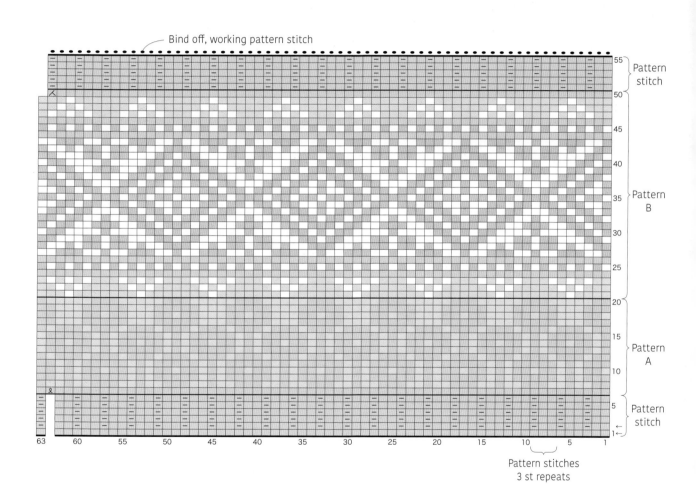

Bind off, working pattern stitch

Pattern stitch

Pattern B

Pattern A

Pattern stitch

Pattern stitches
3 st repeats

NO. 15 Page 27

FINISHED SIZE
Calf circumference 26 cm
Length 33.5 cm

INSTRUCTIONS
Cast on in the standard way, work the leg warmers in the round using pattern stitch and patterns A, B, and A', and then bind off.

YARNS USED
Jamiesons of Shetland Spindrift
Navy (Admiral Navy) (727) 35 g
Off White (Natural White) (104) 20 g
Chocolate (Moorland) (195) 20 g
Gray (Sholmit) (103) 15 g

TOOLS
4 x size 4 (3.3 mm) double pointed needles (DPNs),
4 x size 2 (2.7 mm) double pointed needles (DPNs)

GAUGE (10 cm2)
Patterns A, B, and A' 31 sts 35 rows

LEG WARMERS

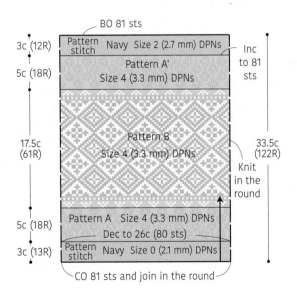

* Refer to the pattern A, B and A' for the color assignments.

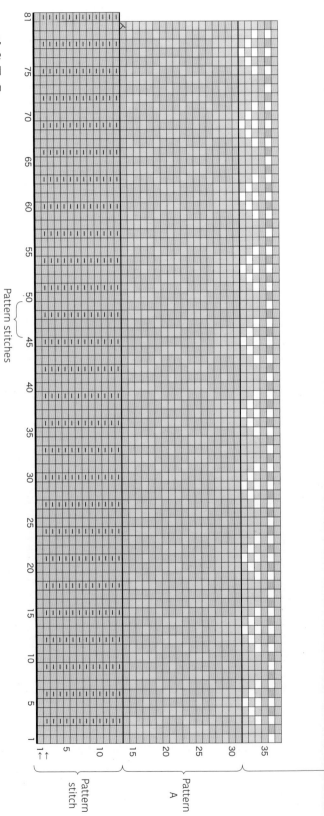

LEG WARMERS PATTERN

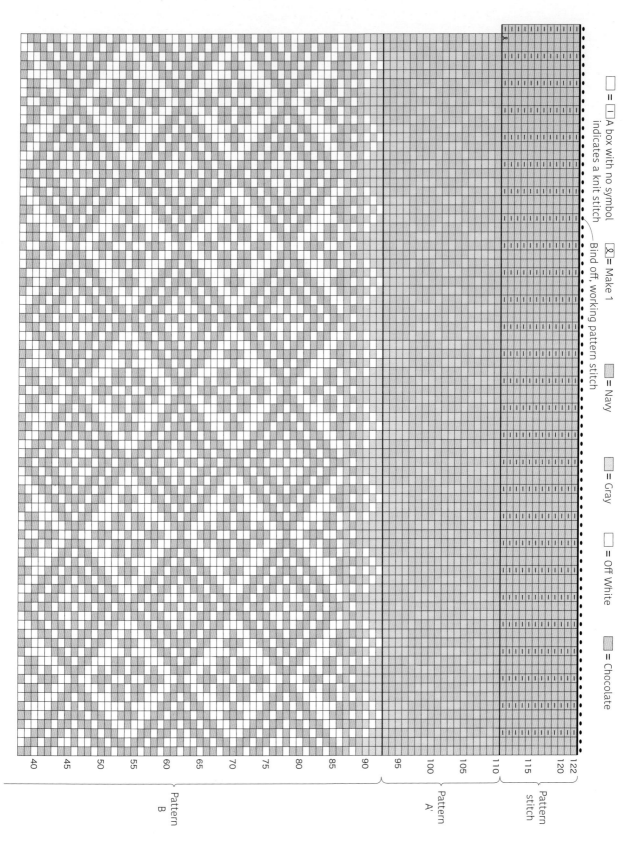

= ☐ A box with no symbol indicates a knit stitch

Ⴃ = Make 1

= Navy

= Gray

= Off White

= Chocolate

Bind off, working pattern stitch

Pattern B

Pattern A'

Pattern stitch

40 45 50 55 60 65 70 75 80 85 90 95 100 105 110 115 120 122

YARNS USED
DARUMA Genmou Ni Chikai Merino Wool
Light Gray (8) 110 g
Light Beige (2) 30 g
Citrus (6) 30 g
Navy (14) 30 g

TOOLS
4 x size 6 (3.9 mm) double pointed
needles (DPNs),

4 x size 4 (3.3 mm) double pointed
needles (DPNs) and

1 x size 2 (2.7 mm) DPN or straight
needle (for binding off).

GAUGE (10 cm²)
Pattern 28 sts 27 rows

FINISHED SIZE
Width 11.5 cm Length 161 cm

INSTRUCTIONS
Cast on in the standard way, work the
muffler in the round using pattern stitch
and the pattern, and then bind off.

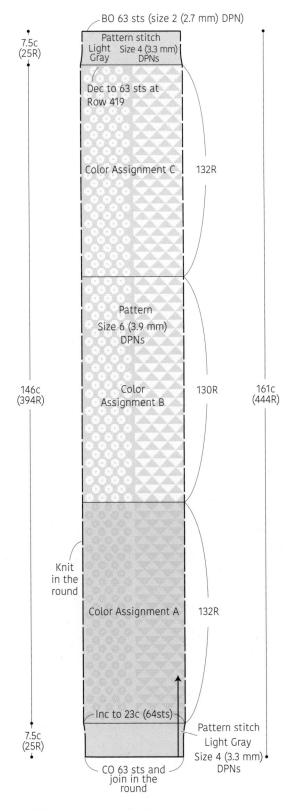

* Refer to the pattern for the color assignments.

SCARF PATTERN

□ = I A box with no symbol indicates a knit stitch   Ω = Make 1   ▨ = Light Gray   ▨ = Navy   ▨ = Light Beige   □ = Citrus

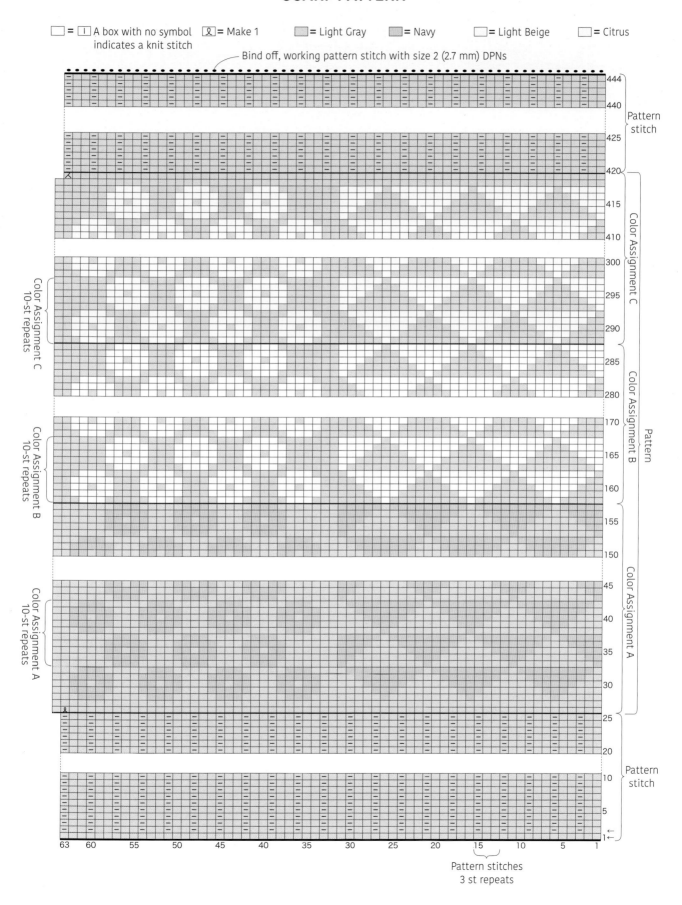

Bind off, working pattern stitch with size 2 (2.7 mm) DPNs

Pattern stitch

Pattern

Color Assignment C
Color Assignment C 10-st repeats

Color Assignment B
Color Assignment B 10-st repeats

Color Assignment A
Color Assignment A 10-st repeats

Pattern stitch

444
440
425
420
415
410
300
295
290
285
280
170
165
160
155
150
45
40
35
30
25
20
10
5
1

63 60 55 50 45 40 35 30 25 20 15 10 5 1

Pattern stitches
3 st repeats

NO. 17 A-K Page 30

a Mitten (x 1)
Size 0 (2.1 mm) DPNs

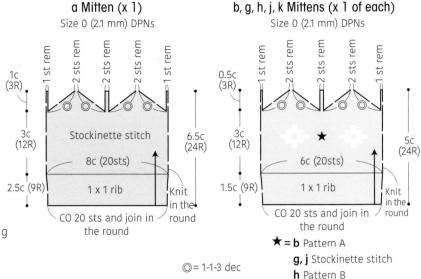

1 st rem / 2 sts rem / 2 sts rem / 2 sts rem / 1 st rem

1c (3R)
3c (12R)
2.5c (9R)

6.5c (24R)

Stockinette stitch
8c (20sts)
1 x 1 rib

CO 20 sts and join in the round

Knit in the round

◎ = 1-1-3 dec

b, g, h, j, k Mittens (x 1 of each)
Size 0 (2.1 mm) DPNs

1 st rem / 2 sts rem / 2 sts rem / 2 sts rem / 1 st rem

0.5c (3R)
3c (12R)
1.5c (9R)

5c (24R)

★
6c (20sts)
1 x 1 rib

CO 20 sts and join in the round

Knit in the round

★ = **b** Pattern A
g, j Stockinette stitch
h Pattern B
k Pattern C

c,i Mittens (x 1 of each)
Size 0 (2.1 mm) DPNs

1 st rem / 2 sts rem / 2 sts rem / 2 sts rem / 1 st rem

1c (3R)
3c (12R)
2.5c (9R)

6.5c (24R)

c Pattern B
i Pattern A
7c (20sts)
1 x 1 rib

CO 20 sts and join in the round

Knit in the round

d,e,f Mittens (x 1 of each)
Size 0 (2.1 mm) DPNs

1 st rem / 2 sts rem / 2 sts rem / 2 sts rem / 1 st rem

0.5c (3R)
3c (12R)
2c (9R)

5.5c (24R)

d Pattern C
e,f Stockinette stitch
7c (20sts)
1 x 1 rib

CO 20 sts and join in the round

Knit in the round

* Refer to the pattern for where to pick up the thumb.
* Refer to the pattern for the color assignments
* Different yarn thicknesses will produce different finished sizes even if you keep the same number of stitches, rows, and needle sizes.

YARNS USED

a. Hamanaka Sonomono Tweed
Ecru (71) 5g

b. Jamieson's of Shetland Spindrift
Blue (Royal) 2g Ecru (Eesit/White) (120) 1g

c. DARUMA Shetland Wool
Red (10) 2g Ecru (1) 1g

d. DARUMA Airy Wool Alpaca
Navy (6) 2g Ecru (1) 1g

e. DARUMA Airy Wool Alpaca
Blue Gray (5) 2g

f. DARUMA Genmou Ni Chikai Merino Wool
Citrus (6) 3g

g. Jamieson's of Shetland Spindrift
Dark Pink (Redcurrant) (572) 2g

h. Jamieson's of Shetland Spindrift
Dark Brown (Espresso) (970) 2g Ecru (Eesit/White) (120) 1g

i. DARUMA Shetland Wool
Ecru (1) 3 g Navy (5) 1g

j. Jamieson's of Shetland Spindrift
Turquioise (Sage) (766) 2g

k. Jamieson's of Shetland Spindrift
Ecru (Eesit/White) (120) 1g Green (Leaf) (788) 1g

TOOLS
5 x size 0 (2.1 mm) double pointed needles (DPNs)

GAUGE (10 cm²)
a Stockinette stitch 25 sts 38 rows

b, g, h, j, k Stockinette stitch, Patterns A, B, C 33 sts 40 rows

c, i Patterns A, B 28.5 sts 37.5 rows

d, e, f Stockinette stitch, pattern C 28 sts 40 rows

FINISHED SIZE (EXCLUDING THE LOOP)
a 4 cm across 6.5 cm long

b, g, h, j, k 3 cm across 5cm long

c, i 3.5 cm across 6.5 cm long

d, e, f 3.5 cm across 5.5 cm long

Thumb
Stockinette stitch Size 0 (2.1 mm) DPNs

8 sts rem

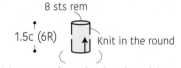

1.5c (6R) Knit in the round

Pick up 8 sts from the thumb position
*Knit **b**, **c**, **d**, **h**, **i** in color A and **k** in color B.

INSTRUCTIONS
1. Cast on in the standard way, work the mittens in the round using 1 x 1 rib and the stitch given in each case, and then fasten off.

2. Pick up the stitch from the mittens, work the thumb in the round with stockinette stitch, and then fasten off.

3. Make the string and shape it into a loop.

a, e, f, g, j Mitten Pattern

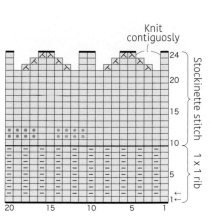

Knit contiguosly

Stockinette stitch

1 x 1 rib

•= f, g, j thumb pick-up point

•= i thumb pick-up point

b, i Mitten Pattern

☐ = Color A   ☐ = Color B

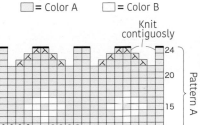

Knit contiguosly

Pattern A

1 x 1 rib

• = a, e thumb pick-up point

• = thumb pick-up point

c, h Mitten Pattern

☐ = Color A   ☐ = Color B

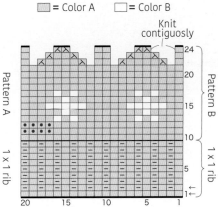

Knit contiguosly

Pattern B

1 x 1 rib

• = b thumb pick-up point

d, k Mitten Pattern

☐ = Color A ☐ = Color B

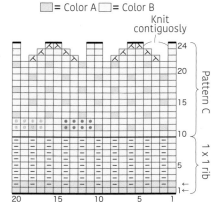

Knit contiguosly

Pattern C

1 x 1 rib

• = d thumb pick-up point

• = k thumb pick-up point

☐ = ☐ A box with no symbol indicates a knit stitch

Color Assignments

	b	c	d	h	i	k
Color A	Blue	Red	Ecru	Dark Brown	Ecru	Green
Color B	Ecru	Ecru	Navy	Ecru	Navy	Ecru

Thumb Pattern
Same for **a** to **k**

Finishing off

Make a string in your preferred length and shape it into a loop

Fasten off the finger tips

How To Make A String

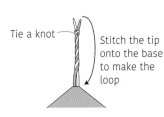

Tie a knot

Stitch the tip onto the base to make the loop

1. Leave some length in the tail of the yarn that you've finished knitting or have fastened off and pull it through the top.

* If you're working with a single color, take one strand and make it two ply.

2. Secure the mitten with tape or other material to prevent it from moving, take the end of one strand and twist it in the direction of the ply, securing it so that the strands do not come undone. Do the same to the other strand.

3. Make a knot with the ends of the two twisted strands, take your hand off the yarn and remove the tape. The yarns will now combine naturally to form a string.

BASIC TECHNIQUES

Knitting With Straight Needles

Casting On

Standard Cast-On

①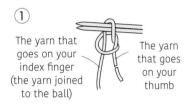

The yarn that goes on your index finger (the yarn joined to the ball)

The yarn that goes on your thumb

Make a loop, leaving a length from the end that is three to four times the width of the stitch, pull the yarn through the loop and hook it over both needles. This will form the first stitch.

②

Hook the yarn onto your left index finger and thumb, holding it in place with the remaining fingers. Hold down the first stitch with your right index finger.

③

Insert the needles through the yarn on the outside of the thumb to hook it on, as shown by the arrow.

④

Insert the needles through the yarn on your index finger as shown by the arrow.

⑤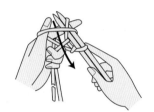

Pull the yarn on your index finger toward you and out through the loop over the thumb.

⑥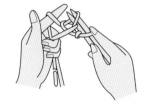

Slip off the yarn around the thumb.

⑦

Put your thumb from in to out through the yarn that has come off your thumb and pull it tight. Repeat steps 3 to 7.

⑧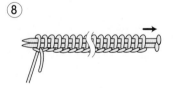

When you have the stitches you need, remove one of the needles.

These cast-on stitches will count as the first row.

- -

Casting On and Joining In The Round

①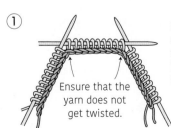

Ensure that the yarn does not get twisted.

Divide the cast-on stitches over three of the needles (or four if you are using five needles).

②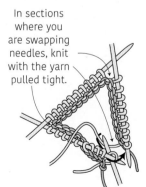

In sections where you are swapping needles, knit with the yarn pulled tight.

Work on with the remaining needle.

KNITTING SYMBOL GUIDE

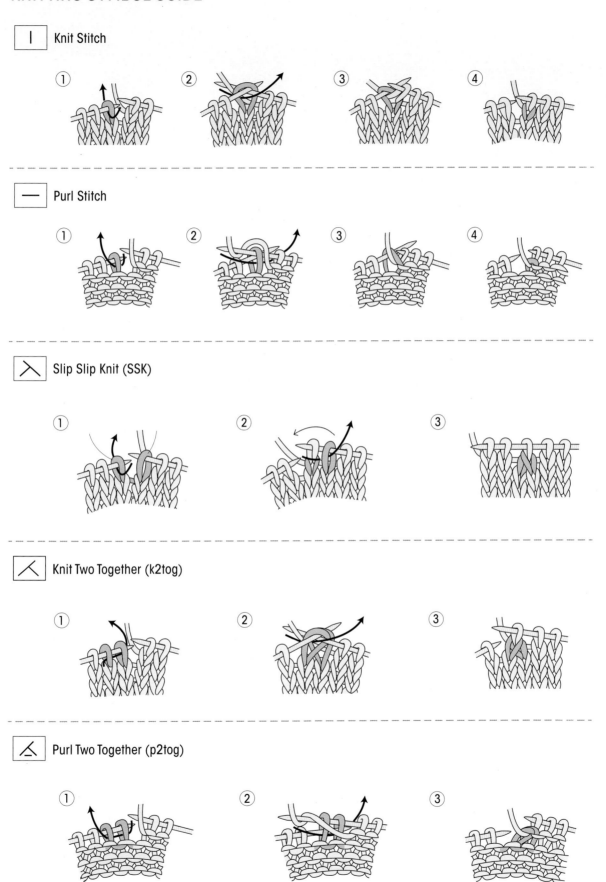

| | Knit Stitch

— Purl Stitch

⟋ Slip Slip Knit (SSK)

⟋ Knit Two Together (k2tog)

⟍ Purl Two Together (p2tog)

◯ Yarn Over

①

Slip the yarn onto the right-hand needle as shown by the arrow.

②

This how it looks with the yarn slipped on. The yarn you have slipped on will form the yarn over.

③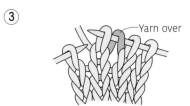

Yarn over

This is how it will look when you have knit the next stitch.

Ω Knit Through Back Loop

① ②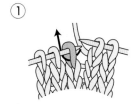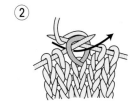

Insert the needle so that the stitch in the row before gets twisted round, and then make a knit stitch.

Ω Make 1

① ②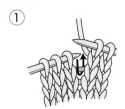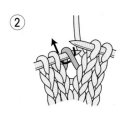

Insert the needle so that the stitch floating across in the row before gets scooped up and twisted round, and then make a knit stitch.

> * Knit through back loop and Make 1 are indicated by the same symbol.
> The stitch is a M1 if the stitches are being increased on the pattern, and a ktbl if they are note.

∨ Slip Stitch
For Edge Stitches

① ②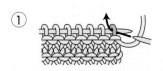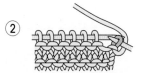

Insert the right-hand needle into the stitch on the lefthand needle as shown by the arrow and transfer it without making a stitch.

Bring the yarn from front to back, and make the next stitch.

For Stitches In Mid-Knit

① ②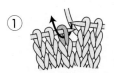

Insert the right-hand needle into the stitch on the left-hand needle as shown by the arrow and transfer it without making a stitch.

This is how the finished slip stitch will look with the yarn brought from the front to the back of the stitch you have transferred onto the right-hand needle.

How To Join New Yarn In Striped Patterns

①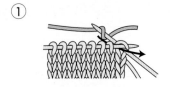

②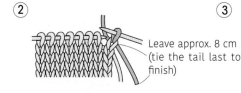

Leave approx. 8 cm (tie the tail last to finish)

③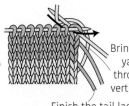

Bring the yarn through vertically

Finish the tail last

Patterns (how the yarn floats to the wrong side)... P. 42

Knitting the thumb position on mittens pp.46, 48

BINDING and FASTENING OFF

 Binding Off   You will need four to five times as much yarn as the width you are binding off.

①

Knit two.

②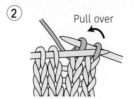

Pull over

Insert the left-hand needle in the first stitch and pull it over the second.

③

Knit one stitch and repeat step 2.

④

Loop the yarn through the last stitch and pull tight.

Fastening Off

①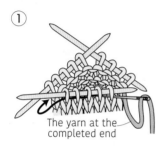

The yarn at the completed end

Thread the yarn through the last row of stitches.

②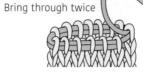

Bring through twice

Bring the yarn through again.

③

Pull the yarn to close the hole, thread the yarn to the wrong side through the knit fabric and cut it off.

Other Basic Techniques

Making A Pompom

①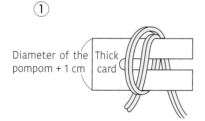

Diameter of the pompom + 1 cm | Thick card

Wrap round the number of times given in the instructions. Tie a knot around the middle and pull tight.

②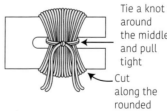

Tie a knot around the middle and pull tight

Cut along the rounded section

③

The result is a neat, round shape.

Attaching Buttons

①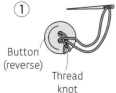

Button (reverse)

Thread knot

②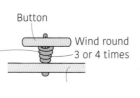

Button

Judge the length of the end of the yarn by the thickness of the knit fabric

Wind round 3 or 4 times

Blind Stitch

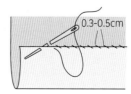

0.3-0.5cm

Tuva Publishing
www.tuvapublishing.com

Address Merkez Mah. Cavusbasi Cad.
No71 Cekmekoy - Istanbul 34782 / Turkey

Tel +9 0216 642 62 62

Knit Latvian Mittens

First Print 2023 / October

All Global Copyrights Belong To
Tuva Tekstil ve Yayıncılık Ltd.

 TuvaYayincilik   TuvaPublishing
 TuvaYayincilik   TuvaPublishing

Content Knit

Editor in Chief
Ayhan DEMİRPEHLİVAN

Project Editor
Kader DEMİRPEHLİVAN

Author
Motoko ISHIKAWA

Technical Editor
Leyla ARAS

Graphic Designers
Ömer ALP, Abdullah BAYRAKÇI,
Tarık TOKGÖZ, Yunus GÜLDOĞAN

ISBN 978-605-7834-75-1

Lady Boutique Series No.8189
Mitten-ya san no Teamino Mitten to Komono
Copyright © Boutique-sha, Inc. 2021
Original Japanese edition published in
Japan by Boutique-sha, Inc.

English translation rights arranged with
Boutique-sha, Inc.